Immigration and the City

Immigration & Society series

Carl L. Bankston III, *Immigrant Networks and Social Capital*

Stephanie A. Bohon & Meghan Conley, *Immigration and Population*

Caroline B. Brettell, *Gender and Migration*

Thomas Faist, Margit Fauser, & Eveline Reisenauer, *Transnational Migration*

Eric Fong & Brent Berry, *Immigration and the City*

Christian Joppke, *Citizenship and Immigration*

Grace Kao, Elizabeth Vaquera, & Kimberly Goyette, *Education and Immigration*

Nazli Kibria, Cara Bowman, & Megan O'Leary, *Race and Immigration*

Peter Kivisto, *Religion and Immigration*

Cecilia Menjívar, Leisy J. Abrego, & Leah C. Schmalzbauer, *Immigrant Families*

Ronald L. Mize & Grace Peña Delgado, *Latino Immigrants in the United States*

Philip Q. Yang, *Asian Immigration to the United States*

Min Zhou & Carl L. Bankston III, *The Rise of the New Second Generation*

Immigration and the City

Eric Fong and Brent Berry

polity

First published in 2017 by Polity Press

Polity Press
65 Bridge Street
Cambridge CB2 1UR, UK

Polity Press
350 Main Street
Malden, MA 02148, USA

ISBN-13: 978-0-7456-9001-8
ISBN-13: 978-0-7456-9002-5(pb)

A catalogue record for this book is available from the British Library.

Library of Congress Cataloging-in-Publication Data
Names: Fong, Eric, 1960- author. | Berry, Brent Matthew, author.
Title: Immigration and the city / Eric Fong, Brent Berry.
Description: Cambridge, UK ; Malden, MA : Polity Press, 2017. | Includes bibliographical references and index.
Identifiers: LCCN 2016029977 (print) | LCCN 2016039542 (ebook) | ISBN 9780745690018 (hardback) | ISBN 9780745690025 (pbk.) | ISBN 9780745690032 (EPdf) | ISBN 9780745690049 (mobi) | ISBN 9780745690056 (Epub)
Subjects: LCSH: Cities and towns. | Emigration and immigration--Social aspects. | Immigrants--Social conditions. | Sociology, Urban.
Classification: LCC HT215 .F66 2017 (print) | LCC HT215 (ebook) | DDC 307.76--dc23
LC record available at https://lccn.loc.gov/2016029977

Typeset in 11 on 13 pt Sabon by Servis Filmsetting Ltd, Stockport, Cheshire
Printed and bound in the United Kingdom by Clays Ltd, St Ives PLC

For further information on Polity, visit our website: www.politybooks.com

Contents

Acknowledgments

Eric Fong would like to thank Kumiko Shibuya for her valuable suggestions. Brent Berry would like to thank Milos Brocic for his outstanding research assistance with the topics of immigrant housing, leisure, and time use in cities.

1

Introduction

We are living in an "age of migration" (Castles et al. 2013). In 2011, about 6 million people in Canada were foreign-born, representing 21 percent of the total population (Statistics Canada 2013). In 2010, about 39 million people in the United States were foreign-born, representing 13 percent of the total population (Singer 2013). Most immigrants settle in cities when they first arrive. This is not a surprising pattern, as the majority of the Canadian and American populations reside in urban areas: 82 percent of the population of Canada and 81 percent of the population of the United States (World Bank 2015). Although many countries have experienced tremendous growth in immigration, this book largely focuses on the settlement and acculturation of immigrants in Canada and the United States. Rich data related to immigration are available in both countries, enabling effective comparisons.

Most people know a little about the settlement patterns of immigrants in cities from discussion with friends and media reports. This book explores these patterns, specifically how geographic contexts shape the settlement patterns of immigrants in contemporary cities. It also explores key aspects of immigrant housing attainment; community, business, and economic activity; and contributions to cosmopolitan city life. The settlement patterns, community forms, and economic endeavors of immigrants have become more varied and dispersed in contemporary cities, so a "one-size-fits-all" approach to explaining adaptation of immigrants in cities is no longer appropriate. Social scientists have been forced to expand and qualify their descriptions of these patterns, and also to use new forms of evidence, such as time-use data, to understand the behaviors of immigrants.

Understanding the social and economic lives of immigrants in cities is an important topic, and requires two processes to be clarified simultaneously: how immigrants adjust to the social, cultural, and economic environment of the city, and how they contribute to the social, cultural, and economic development of the city.

Characteristics of Contemporary Immigration

Many immigrants living in Canada and the United States arrived after 1970 as a result of changes in immigration policies. This new wave of immigrants has two major characteristics. First, many now come from non-European countries. The 2011 National Household Survey in Canada revealed that about 10 percent of immigrants in Canada were from African countries and nearly 60 percent were from Asian countries, especially the Philippines, China, and India, which represented 13 percent, 11 percent, and 10 percent of the total immigrant population respectively (Statistics Canada 2013). In 2013, most immigrants in the United States were from Mexico, at 28 percent of the total immigrant population, followed by India and China at 5 percent each, and then the Philippines at 4 percent (Zong and Batalova 2015). Because most of these immigrants chose to settle in major cities, one major direct consequence is the increasing racial diversity of cities, so the processes of immigrant integration may differ from those of European immigrants in previous generations.

The second characteristic is the increasing socioeconomic disparity among immigrants: some arrive with limited language and education, while others may have completed higher education and have considerable financial resources. In 2013, about 50 percent of immigrants aged 5 or older in the United States reportedly spoke English "not at all," "not well," or "well," and about 50 percent only spoke English or spoke English "very well." Additionally, about 30 percent of immigrants did not have a high school diploma, while 28 percent had completed a university degree (Zong and Batalova 2015). According to the 2011 Canadian National Household Survey, about 5 percent of immigrants aged 25–64 in Canada were not able to hold a conversation in either English or French; about 12 percent did not have a high school diploma, while about 31 percent had completed a university degree. These differences shape diverse integration outcomes: some immigrants have more resources to help them adapt, and more residential options. Because socioeconomic differences can lead to diverse assimilation outcomes, not all immigrants go through the same processes of integration.

Characteristics of the Urban Context

Since the 1970s, there have also been unique developments in the urban contexts where immigrants settle. Most major cities underwent rapid suburbanization between 1950 and 1970. Cities became more dispersed and decentralized, and a larger proportion of the population in urban areas settled in the suburbs. In 2006, Statistics Canada estimated that only 48 percent of the population in all metropolitan areas lived in neighborhoods less than 10 kilometers from the city center (Turcotte 2008). Suburban sprawl is known to affect daily activities and group interactions. The scattered residential arrangements of suburban areas encourage automobile culture, weakening close networks among neighbors and neighborhood shops. Suburban sprawl also usually means more distance between residence and workplace. Additionally, most suburban households are middle class, suggesting a possible socioeconomic segregation from people living in the city center.

The economies of cities have also changed to benefit more educated immigrants working in globally connected businesses at the expense of low-skill immigrants working in traditional manufacturing jobs. Since the 1970s, many manufacturing jobs have moved to developing countries. In the United States, for example, Chicago lost 177,000 manufacturing jobs and Detroit lost 87,000 between 1995 and 2005 (Pacione 2009). In Canada, the percentage of manufacturing jobs dropped from 22 percent to 17 percent of all jobs in only five years, from 1975 to 1980. Low-skill immigrants have been seriously affected, because manufacturing jobs are their major source of employment. At the same time, demand for skilled workers has increased.

This book explores immigrant settlement patterns within this increasingly complex context: how do urban forms shape the integration patterns of immigrants, and how does the adaptation of immigrants change urban forms?

Chapter 2 focuses on an issue central to understanding immigration and the city: the residential patterns of immigrants. It summarizes the classic perspectives and explores how scholars have recently developed new perspectives in an attempt to address some of the limitations of the classic perspectives. Almost all these theoretical perspectives suggest that the residential patterns of immigrants reflect their adaptation. In other words, their adaptation to the new country shapes urban forms. Chapter 2 also reviews the findings from current studies, which clearly show that no single perspective can be applied to all immigrant groups. Finally, it focuses on four types of neighborhoods that have been largely shaped by the process and outcomes of immigrant integration: mixed, gentrified, economically polarized, and immigrant suburban.

Chapter 3 focuses on the attainment of housing by immigrants at the individual level. It presents different trajectories of housing attainment related to individual socioeconomic resources. The discussion will reveal how immigrants with different socioeconomic resources adapt to the existing urban context. It will also show how the development of the physical housing environment is shaped by the socioeconomic and demographic background of immigrants. Overall, immigrants with different socioeconomic resources have diverse paths to housing attainment.

Chapter 4 focuses on immigrant community: the social and economic activities that bind immigrants together. Specifically, how have changes in the socioeconomic backgrounds of immigrants led to changes in the membership and functions of the community? The discussion will reveal that immigrant communities are beneficial to not only the first generation, but also the second generation. Chapter 4 also presents a review of two recent urban developments: the concentration of immigrants in suburban areas, and the transnational dimensions of immigrant communities. It will explore how the adaptation of immigrants transforms urban patterns, and how the nature and functions of immigrant communities are becoming more complex.

Chapter 5 focuses on immigrant businesses. Economic activities are one of the major activities of immigrant communities in cities. To help clarify the concentration of immigrant businesses, it presents a few ways to capture the complexity of contemporary economic activities among immigrants. As immigrant businesses become more diverse in size and involved in different industrial sectors, their geographical distribution is affected. Additionally, city contexts shape the earnings of individuals involved in immigrant businesses.

Chapter 6 explores the presence of immigrants in relation to the culture of the city. First, it focuses on how the food offered in local restaurants is influenced by immigrant communities and how the status of ethnic cuisine is elevated. Second, it explores how the socioeconomic background of immigrants shapes their participation in different leisure sports. Finally, it reviews how the cultural practices of immigrants shape the suburban landscape and public spaces.

Chapter 7 addresses the need for different types of data in research about the increasing complexity of immigrant adaptation and its relationship to urban patterns. It illustrates how time-use data can help clarify immigrant adaptation in a city. These data provide detailed information about individuals, so they reveal how people spend their time and how these patterns shape integration patterns, which in turn can lead to different urban forms.

2

The Residential Patterns of Immigrants in Cities

Immigrant neighborhoods can be found in most large North American cities, such as New York, San Francisco, Toronto, and Vancouver. For example, we see Chinese immigrants in Diamond Bar, Los Angeles County, California; Salvadoran immigrants in Mount Pleasant, Washington, DC; Korean immigrants in Palisades Park, Bergen County, New Jersey; and Asian immigrants in Brampton, Ontario, Canada. In these neighborhoods, ethnic signage is everywhere. It is common to hear people speaking their own ethnic languages and see them dressed in distinctive ethnic clothing. Some of these neighborhoods were developed long ago by earlier generations, but others have only recently become associated with an ethnic group.

Why Study Immigrants' Residential Patterns?

For decades, researchers have sought to identify the residential patterns of immigrants and to explain the causes, perpetuation, and consequences of these patterns (Farley and Allen 1990; Frey and Farley 1996; Iceland and Scopilliti 2008; Lieberson 1963; Massey and Denton 1990). Some studies have focused on all immigrants together, while others have focused on particular groups (Fong and Hou 2009; Iceland and Scopilliti 2008; Massey and Denton 1988a). The term "immigrant residential segregation" usually refers to the physical separation of immigrants from non-immigrants (Lieberson 1963). Immigrant residential segregation occurs when immigrants are not evenly distributed across a city's neighborhoods; this unevenness can be mild or extreme. Patterns of segregation can be further characterized by examining how immigrants vary from the general population in terms of demographic and socioeconomic variables.

What are the social implications of immigrant residential segregation? Some studies have concluded that opportunities in life are strongly related to residential location (Massey and Fong 1990; Massey et al. 1987; Ramey 2013; Schieman 2005; Villarreal and Silva 2006). For example, neighborhoods with lower socioeconomic standing are usually associated with lower school completion rates (Massey et al. 2006), less access to job information (Smith 2005; Wilson 1996), higher rates of unemployment (Wilson 1996), and poorer physical health among residents (Hou and Myles 2005; Schieman 2005). Neighborhoods with low socioeconomic standing also have fewer good schools (Smith et al. 1997), worse physical amenities (Massey and Fong 1990), and more exposure to criminal activity (Sampson 2012; Sampson et al. 1997). Therefore, immigrant groups that are segregated into neighborhoods with low socioeconomic standing are likely to face greater challenges in terms of social and economic disadvantages.

For immigrants living in segregated neighborhoods, even affluent neighborhoods, social isolation is a hurdle to achieving full integration into the new society. Insufficient opportunities to interact with the local-born population limits the diversity of social networks and delays learning about the new culture and environment (Alba and Nee 2003; Massey and Mullan 1984; Massey et al. 1987). This social isolation effect can have a lasting impact, not only for the first generation, but also for children of immigrants. Zhou (1997) suggested that immigrant segregation in poor neighborhoods can inhibit the integration of second-generation immigrants: the children of immigrants living in poor neighborhoods are deprived of social and economic resources, such as better schools and access to good job information from neighbors. The social environment of these neighborhoods fosters social deprivation, which in turn may promote an "oppositional culture" among members of the younger generation who feel abandoned by society (Ogbu 2008). They may be skeptical of the ability of school achievement to provide upward mobility and have little hope of ever joining the middle class.

How to Measure Residential Segregation

Scholars have proposed many measures of residential segregation, but no single measure conceptually captures the five distinctive dimensions of segregation that have been identified: evenness, exposure, concentration, centralization, and clustering (Massey and Denton 1988b). "Evenness" is the extent to which the distribution of two groups living within geographic units in a city reflects their overall citywide proportions. In the ideal case, an "even" distribution of two groups means that the proportion of the two groups in each neighborhood is the same as the proportion in the entire city. "Exposure" refers to the possibility of interaction between two groups in geographic units in a city based on their relative proportions. This is not based on deviation from the ideal of "evenness." A high exposure refers to the high likelihood of a group member who is "experiencing segregation" (Massey and Denton 1988b) being exposed to members of another group living in the same neighborhood. Thus, exposure is affected by the sizes of the two groups being compared. "Concentration" refers to the relative amount of space occupied by members of a group (Massey and Denton 1988b). Concentration can be absolute or relative. Absolute concentration refers to the area occupied by a group, whereby a group occupying a smaller area is more concentrated, whereas relative concentration takes into consideration the concentration of the other group. "Centralization" refers to the level at which a group resides in or near the central area of the city. It can also be absolute or relative. Absolute centralization refers to the proportion of the group occupying the central area, while relative concentration refers to the proportion of the group that would need to move to match the centralization of a different group. "Clustering" refers to the extent to which members of a group reside in geographic units that are adjacent to one another. Similarly, clustering level includes two types of measures. Absolute clustering refers to the average proportion of groups living near each other. Relative clustering refers to the average distance between members of a group, compared with the average distance between members of another group.

Among the various indexes that have been proposed to measure these five dimensions of segregation, the dissimilarity index (D) and the interaction index (P^*) are the most often used. These measures are easy to compute and interpret, but require simplifying the population into two groups, which can mean that important multi-group dynamics are overlooked (Fong and Shibuya 2005).

Most American and Canadian studies about the residential patterns of immigrants use census tracts as a proxy for neighborhoods in calculating the segregation index. A census tract is a geostatistical area designated by a national statistics agency (i.e. US Census Bureau in the US, and Statistics Canada in Canada). In both the United States and Canada, census tracts may include 2,500–8,000 residents, with an average of 4,000 residents. The boundaries are usually stable and follow distinctive physical features, such as major roads and geographic contours. When each census tract was first created, individuals and households within the borders tended to be relatively homogeneous in terms of socioeconomic status, meaning there was less variation within each tract than across tracts.

The Classical Explanations

The analysis of immigrant residential patterns has a long tradition in the social sciences. This section summarizes the classical explanations offered by sociologists in the early twentieth century, a period of rapid urban change as many immigrants arrived in North America from Europe. A group of sociologists, now referred to as the Chicago School, was especially important in setting the foundation for later research.

Ernest Burgess: Concentric Zone Model

Ernest Burgess was a member of the Chicago School, and made one of the most important theoretical contributions to understanding immigrant residential patterns. In his seminal work *The City* (1925), he introduced his Concentric Zone Model to explain immigrant residential patterns. According to this theory, cities expand in a series of concentric circles. Burgess had observed that in Chicago, immigrants first settled in a zone with deteriorating housing mixed with factories, adjacent to the "central business district." He labeled this area "the zone in transition." Immigrants settled in this area because housing values were low and the area was close to their place of work; they clustered in these neighborhoods because they had limited resources upon arrival. As they stayed in the country longer and accumulated more economic resources, they moved into what Burgess called the "zone of workingmen's homes," which was next to the zone of transition and generally included two-parent family homes. Outside the zone of workingmen's homes was "the zone of better residence." This zone typically consisted of residences with spacious lots for middle-class families. The most outward zone was "the commuters' zone," located at the boundary of the city, with still better housing. Immigrants are assumed to move outward to better housing areas as their socioeconomic resources improve.

Louis Wirth was a contemporary of Burgess and was also a key member of the Chicago School. His work focused on Jewish settlement in the United States during the early twentieth century (1962). He made major contributions to research about immigrant communities, which will be discussed in more detail in chapter 4. Briefly, Wirth was influenced by Burgess's arguments, and assumed that the early Jewish residential segregation was temporary and would gradually disappear. He speculated that Jews would move away from ethnically concentrated areas and into better neighborhoods if their economic resources improved and if neighborhoods were available.

More recently, scholars have questioned the applicability of

Burgess's concentric model to other cities and time periods (Berry and Rees 1969; Scott 2000). His model was certainly appropriate for Chicago in the 1920s, but while subsequent research has largely supported his theory in terms of neighborhoods being differentiated by socioeconomic and demographic characteristics, the differentiation seldom occurs in the form of concentric zones (Janson 1980; Logan and Molotch 2007; White 1988).

Despite these criticisms, Burgess's attempt to link immigrant adaptation with urban form had several major implications that transcend historical specificity. First, he used a simple model to link the two most important dimensions for studying human behavior – space and time – in understanding the experiences of immigrants in the city. His argument provides the basic premise for understanding immigrant residential patterns over time. Second, he identified the very important role of socioeconomic resources in the residential patterns of immigrants, arguing that residential location largely reflects the economic standing of immigrants. His argument was based on two assumptions: less desirable neighborhoods are associated with lower housing values; and immigrants, like other citizens, will move to better neighborhoods if their economic resources improve. Third, he postulated that all immigrants would prefer to share neighborhoods with other groups if economic resources allow. Together, these three aspects of Burgess's work continue to influence contemporary interpretations of the residential patterns of immigrants.

Walter Firey: Sentiment and Symbolism

Walter Firey disagreed with Burgess and provided an alternative perspective for understanding immigrant residential patterns (1945). He argued that in addition to the economic exchange value, residential locations have cultural value: all space is associated with cultural values that in turn can affect people's choice of location. His analysis focused on two neighborhoods in Boston: an upper-class neighborhood known as Boston Common, and a lower-class Italian neighborhood called North End. He concluded that Italians prefer living near other family members; even members of younger generations that are well assimilated prefer to live with, or in close proximity to, family. Additionally, given their strong social ties, the presence of ethnic organizations, and the celebration of traditional festivals, Italians of different generations are motivated to stay in their ethnic neighborhood despite improvements in their economic resources.

In summary, Firey identified the critical role played by the social dimension in the residential patterns of immigrants. Immigrants and their descendants may continue to live near each other not only because of economic constraints, but also because of social activities and supports among co-ethnic members. The significance of the social dimension adds to the complexity of understanding immigrant residential patterns.

Recent Theoretical Developments

More recently, William Julius Wilson (Wilson 1987; 1996) focused on urban poverty concentration and Douglas Massey and his colleagues (Eggers and Massey 1991; Massey and Denton 1990; Massey et al. 1994) focused on residential segregation patterns among Blacks in large cities in the United States. Their research has renewed interest in understanding how neighborhoods shape the social and economic outcomes of their residents. Three key models have been developed to explain contemporary residential patterns: spatial assimilation, place stratification, and individual preference.

Spatial Assimilation Model

Clarifying residential patterns is a key component of understanding the processes of assimilation and stratification. However, from Robert Park's (1936a) work on the race relations cycle to Milton Gordon's (1964) work on the dimensions of assimilation, the spatial dimension was discussed only marginally. More recently, Douglas Massey and his colleagues demonstrated that sharing neighborhoods with other groups is a crucial aspect of assimilation: "Assimilation does not occur in a vacuum. Groups and individuals interact in a physical world. Spatial assimilation is usually viewed as a necessary intermediate step between acculturation and other types of assimilation. Spatial elements strongly affect nearly all stages of assimilation subsequent to acculturation" (Massey and Mullan 1984: 837).

Spatial assimilation is defined as a process by which groups share neighborhoods and live in close proximity. It is an important indicator of social mobility, and moving from one neighborhood to another reflects a group's experience of social mobility. Because residential locations vary in terms of housing costs, and better quality housing is associated with higher housing value, then individual immigrants with more resources can afford more residential choices. At the same time, neighborhoods with better amenities, schools, and social institutions improve opportunities for residents. Thus, spatial assimilation is an important step to achieving full integration in society.

Massey and his associates have suggested that spatial assimilation creates two residential patterns (Crowder et al. 2011; 2012; South and Crowder 1997; 1998). They linked social mobility with residential patterns, and suggested that the average socioeconomic status of immigrants should be higher in neighborhoods where they are more likely to come in contact with members of the host society. Conversely, the average socioeconomic level of immigrants should be lower in neighborhoods that are farther away from established neighborhoods of majority members of the host society. For example, immigrants residing in Westwood in Los Angeles, California and Rosedale in Toronto, Ontario, usually have more socioeconomic resources because housing is more expensive there. They also have more opportunities to interact with neighbors from the majority group.

Place Stratification Model

The place stratification model moves beyond explaining residential patterns in terms of socioeconomic status of individuals and the demographic distribution of groups (Alba and Logan 1991). Instead, this model treats different levels of government, real estate, and financial institutions, and other housing-related institutions, as playing critical roles in maintaining racial residential segregation. In "American Apartheid," Massey and Denton (1990) documented how real estate agents steered minority home buyers away from White neighborhoods. Similar patterns of steering minority immigrants toward immigrant neighborhoods have been documented in other immigrant gateway cities, such as Toronto (Fong and Chan 2010). These discriminatory acts treat racial/ethnic minorities "according to their group's relative standing in society, hindering the ability of even the socially mobile members to reside in the same communities as comparable whites" (Alba and Logan, 1993: 1391).

Charles (2006) suggested that these discriminatory acts are related to two variants of racial prejudice. The first type of prejudice stems from conventional prejudice against members of an "outgroup." Unfavorable attitudes and behavior toward members of outgroups is commonly found in society. The second type of prejudice is related to the social status and position of the individuals involved. Members of an advantaged group want to maintain their status and keep a distance from those in a more disadvantaged position, so they act in different ways toward them. Additionally, given that life chances and quality of life continue to be channeled unevenly to groups through spatial arrangements, advantaged groups see the spatial hierarchy as a way of retaining their resources, including the status and prestige associated with their neighborhoods.

Alba and Logan (1991) argued that minority groups face the consequence of limited access to desirable neighborhoods and restricted ability to share neighborhoods with the majority group even when they have socioeconomic resources. This tends to construct and perpetuate hierarchical spatial arrangements, leading to two residential patterns. First, disadvantaged racial and ethnic minorities are less likely to reside in desirable neighborhoods and to share neighborhoods with the majority group. Second, the disadvantaged groups are less able to translate their socioeconomic resources into better neighborhood outcomes.

Recent studies have identified two possible forms of place stratification (Pais and Elliott 2008). In cases of the "weaker" form, disadvantaged groups experience some levels of integration, but majority groups still reside in better neighborhoods and are less likely to share neighborhoods with minorities. In cases of the "stronger" form, disadvantaged groups experience stagnation in residential integration, with no sign of convergence despite socio-economic improvements.

Individual Preference Model

According to the individual preference model, residential patterns reflect differences in preferences for the racial and ethnic composition of neighborhoods. Preference involves two components: the preference to share neighborhoods with one's own group, and the preference to share neighborhoods with other groups (Charles 2006; Clark and Ledwith 2005).

In Canada and the United States, ethnic concentration levels in neighborhoods are no longer related to the acculturation level of immigrant groups. As a result of changes to government immigration policies, many immigrants now arrive with considerable socioeconomic resources and/or high educational levels. Many are able to move right into a desirable location, such as a suburban neighborhood, and many choose to do so (Li 1998b). This means that residential choice is based not on acculturation level or socioeconomic necessity, but on the preference of immigrants according to their taste, such as living close to ethnic religious institutions and familiar cultural organizations (Logan et al. 2002). Changes in the configuration of urban spaces through high-rise development and suburbanization have also made it possible for many ethnic communities to emerge. Instead of using their socioeconomic resources to move into integrated neighborhoods, such as those where residents are predominantly White and local-born, many immigrants choose to live in affluent neighborhoods that are culturally familiar (Myles and Hou 2004). Logan et al. (2002) termed these neighborhoods, where residents have high socioeconomic status and tend to engage in the mainstream labor force, as "ethnic communities." The socioeconomic demographics of the residents of these neighborhoods differ considerably from those of the ethnic neighborhoods described by the early Chicago School.

Residential patterns also are affected by preferences about sharing neighborhoods with other racial groups (Bobo and Zubrinsky 1996; Charles 2001). Different groups tend to have different preferences about the racial and ethnic composition of neighborhoods, which can be viewed as one aspect of the bundle of preferred social amenities in neighborhoods. Individuals must decide how much they are willing to adjust their preference for a particular racial/ethnic composition in a neighborhood in order to gain some other desirable social amenities.

Together, these two preferences for sharing neighborhoods, with one's own group and with other groups, shape the residential patterns of immigrants. If groups prefer to stay with their own group members even after socioeconomic advancement, and prefer to live in highly co-ethnic concentrated areas rather than in neighborhoods with other social amenities, those immigrant groups will usually exhibit high levels of clustering.

Empirical Findings on Residential Segregation of Immigrants

Ample evidence supports the theory that when immigrants arrive in a new country, they usually choose to live among their co-ethnic friends and family members, from whom they can seek assistance and support. The question is whether they gradually move into neighborhoods that are shared with other groups as they stay in the country longer or improve their socioeconomic resources.

The research findings are mixed. On one hand, some studies support the spatial assimilation theory, in which immigrants eventually move away from co-ethnic neighborhoods and into mixed neighborhoods. Based on data from the 2000 American census, Alba and Nee (2003) concluded that the residential dispersion of Latino and Asian immigrants over generations is well documented. Iceland and Scopilliti (2008) came to a similar conclusion based on data from the 1990 and 2000 American census; they found clear patterns of Hispanic, Asian, and Black immigrants experiencing higher levels of segregation from native-born non-Hispanic Whites than their native-born counterparts. They also found that recent immigrants had higher levels of residential segregation from native-born Whites than those who arrived earlier. When they focused on specific Hispanic groups, such as Mexicans and Cubans, and specific Asian groups, such as Chinese, Filipinos, and East Indians, and specific Black immigrant groups, such as Jamaicans, Haitians, and Nigerians, they found considerable variations among the groups. The extent and pace of spatial assimilation varied among racial and ethnic immigrant groups, but in general Hispanic and Black immigrant groups tended to experience more segregation despite increases in socioeconomic resources.

Suburbanization is another indicator of integration. Immigrants have become increasingly likely to share neighborhoods with the local-born population. Based on data from the 1970 and 1980 American censuses, Massey and Denton (1988a) found increasing representation of racial/ethnic immigrant minority groups in suburban areas.

Research findings from other countries also support the spatial assimilation model. Fong and Hou (2009) drew from the 2001 Canadian census and found that among Blacks and Asians, both groups having large proportions of immigrants, the proportion of Whites in their neighborhoods increased over successive generations. For example, the average proportion of Whites in the neighborhoods of first-generation South Asians was about 0.47, while for the second generation it was 0.61. The average proportion of Whites in the neighborhoods of average first-generation Black immigrants was 0.56, while for the second generation it was 0.63. Fong and Hou (2009) also found that each successive generation is more efficient than the previous generations in translating their socioeconomic resources. Similar patterns have been observed in major European cities. Andersson (2007) found that immigrants in Sweden were heavily clustered in co-ethnic neighborhoods. Other European research suggests that among immigrants, lower co-ethnic proportions in neighborhoods are associated with higher socioeconomic status (Musterd and Ostendorf 2007).

However, some studies have concluded that some residential patterns are not well explained by the spatial assimilation theory. One obvious example is the persistence of the segregation of Blacks from Whites in the United States. Using census data from 1970 and 1980, Massey and Denton found that Black–White segregation levels in the 30 largest cities remained persistently high despite increases in family income (Massey and Denton 1988a). They also found that the segregation of Blacks in suburban areas was at virtually the same level as in the city. Iceland and Scopilliti (2008) studied Black immigrants in the United States and found that both Black Hispanic and Black non-Hispanic immigrants experienced higher levels of residential segregation than non-Hispanic Asians from native-born non-Hispanic Whites. These patterns were unaffected by their length of residence in the United States. Crowder et al. (2012) explored data from the Panel Study of Income Dynamics and the recent census, and found that Blacks are less likely to move into multi-ethnic neighborhoods, even considering socioeconomic resources. By 2009, the level of residential segregation between Blacks and Whites had declined, but formidable barriers to Black–White social integration remain in the US. One major barrier is preferences about who to share neighborhoods with. Surveys of Detroit and Chicago residents in 2004–2005 revealed that Whites are less likely to want to share their neighborhoods with Blacks than Blacks with Whites (Krysan et al. 2009). Other scholars have suggested that racial steering persists in the housing market, with Black and White real estate agents disproportionately representing properties in Black and White neighborhoods of their own groups, respectively (Kwate et al. 2013). In Canada, both Blacks and Asians, two major immigrant groups, exhibit residential patterns that are inconsistent with the spatial assimilation theory: Fong and Wilkes (1999) found that their socioeconomic resources are not correlated with their likelihood of sharing neighborhoods with Whites.

The decoupling of acculturation and economic resources from ethnic concentration in neighborhoods hints at the role of preference. Immigrants do not necessarily move out of their ethnic neighborhoods even when their economic resources improve. Some groups cluster in neighborhoods that are associated with high economic status. Case studies of groups such as the Chinese in Monterey Park, Los Angeles, show that middle-class immigrants choose to stay in their ethnic community despite socioeconomic improvements (Horton 1995). Additionally, Jewish populations with high levels of socioeconomic resources exhibit considerable residential clustering (Fong and Chan 2011).

Studies have also demonstrated that groups have differential preferences about the ethnic and racial composition of their neighborhoods. Farley and his colleagues (1994) employed an innovative way of understanding racial preferences about neighborhoods among groups by asking whether individuals would be willing to move into neighborhoods with various proportions of Whites. The findings suggested that most Whites did not prefer to move into integrated neighborhoods. About 85 percent of Blacks preferred integrated neighborhoods with 55 percent Blacks. Another study, based on the 1992–4 Multi-City Study of Urban Inequality, found that both Hispanics and Asians prefer integrated neighborhoods, and that Whites are least likely to prefer integrated neighborhoods (Charles 2001).

The desire among minority groups to have a substantial co-ethnic presence in their neighborhoods is strongly related to fears about discrimination and hostility toward their group, whereas preferences for group composition among Whites are more related to worries about cultural differences (Charles 2006).

In short, the findings do not provide clear support for a specific model to explain the residential patterns of all groups. Instead, they demonstrate that the experiences of some groups are better explained by certain models. The models should be applied to various groups with caution.

The following sections discuss four types of neighborhood that have been shaped by the process and outcomes of immigrant integration: mixed, gentrified, economically polarized immigrant, and immigrant suburban. They also help illustrate the complexity of residential patterns among immigrants.

Mixed Neighborhoods

In the late 1960s, changes to immigration policies in Canada and the United States led to large numbers of immigrants from non-European countries. In the 1970s, researchers started to see a new trend in the racial/ethnic composition of neighborhoods. Lee and Wood (1991) analyzed American census data from 1970 and 1980 and found that the succession pattern of neighborhoods changing from White to Black when Blacks begin to move in did not apply in most cities: they documented diverse patterns of succession, including mixed neighborhoods. Drawing from the same set of data, Denton and Massey (1991) found that racial diversity did not lead to racial turnover in neighborhoods. They even identified increasing racial diversity in neighborhoods, and suggested that this might reflect a gradual change in White attitudes about race, or evidence that the 1968 Fair Housing Act had effectively reduced segregation. Based on a longer time frame of census data, from 1980 to 2000, Logan and Zhang (2010) suggested that stable racial diversity was becoming more common in neighborhoods, including those with high socioeconomic status.

Fong (2013) observed similar increasing racial diversity in Canada due to the large influx of immigrants from non-European countries. He found that a considerable proportion of neighborhoods were racially mixed, and that minority immigrants were sharing neighborhoods with White immigrants. Thus, the increasing diversity in neighborhoods does not necessarily equate to an increase in immigrants sharing neighborhoods with local-born populations.

Multi-ethnic neighborhoods foster dynamics that have drawn considerable attention in recent years. Instead of focusing on the relationship between majority and minority groups in neighborhoods, scholars are beginning to explore multi-group relations. Some are focusing on the paths to integration among immigrants living in neighborhoods that have become increasingly diverse (Logan and Zhang 2010). Others are investigating the attitudes that develop toward immigrants in multi-ethnic neighborhoods

(Wu et al. 2011). Still others are exploring the civic participation of immigrants in a multi-ethnic environment (Stoll and Wong 2007).

However, most theoretical models focus on two groups, i.e. the majority–minority relationship, and most indexes used to measure the segregation level are based on the comparison of two groups. Theoretical models and segregation measurements must be updated to accommodate the multi-group context, because this emerging phenomenon challenges the conventional understanding of immigrant adaptation.

Gentrified Neighborhoods

Traditionally, immigrants have settled in inner cities, often in the same neighborhoods later favored by gentrifiers. Gentrification is defined as the shift in an urban community toward wealthier residents and/or businesses; the associated increases in property values contribute to the displacement of immigrants and other residents who rely on affordable housing. Ley (2005) documented the recent spectacular growth of the 'creative class' or white-collar middle-class workforce in once-neglected inner-city neighborhoods that had been settled by immigrants. Echoing Ley's observation, Hwang (2016) showed that the presence of Asian and Hispanic populations is significantly related to gentrification of neighborhoods in 23 major American cities.

Tensions between older immigrant residents and economically and politically stronger new residents have led to a reshaping of landscapes, often in favor of the new residents. A new bourgeois culture marked by new services exemplifying conspicuous consumption has slowly replaced the ethnic businesses operating in these communities (Ley 2005). However, despite the apparent cosmopolitanism of many gentrifiers, many are actually intolerant of diversity (Ray 1998). Furthermore, governments may provide incentives for gentrification, with the goal of changing the character of inner cities to favor development and amenities that are aimed at the interests and wallets of middle-class migrants (Blomley 1997; Zacharias 1997). Because of these multiple factors, in addition to economic barriers, many new immigrants feel unwelcome in gentrifying neighborhoods.

Economically Polarized Immigrant Neighborhoods

Increasing inequalities in income and wealth have influenced the concentrations and distributions of immigrants within cities (Hulchanski 2010). In the United States and Canada, income inequality has increased every decade since the 1970s (Fortin et al. 2012; Maclachlan and Sawada 1997). These increases are amplified at the neighborhood level due to the particularities of the housing markets. For example, Bourne (1997) found that immigrants contribute to the increasing socioeconomic segregation of large urban areas because they are drawn, because of government selection criteria, from increasingly diverse socioeconomic backgrounds: from poor refugees to wealthy economic immigrants. These different subgroups of immigrants live in different communities, and face housing markets that vary considerably in terms of price and rent/ownership (Murdie 2008).

One effect of this increasing social and economic polarization in contemporary multi-ethnic cities is that immigrant groups seek enclaves where they congregate with others from a similar social class and with similar ethno-cultural characteristics. Thus, polarization leads to more polarization, as large cities undergoing sizable immigration experience more segregation, both voluntary and involuntary. Ray (1998) studied these processes of socio-spatial segregation among immigrants in Montreal and Toronto. Partly as a result of their time in Canada and social distance from the mainstream "host" society, immigrants from non-European countries were more concentrated then those from traditional source countries. More specifically, Central American and Vietnamese immigrants were most isolated from the Anglo and French host populations. Conversely, immigrants who self-identified as Black were relatively dispersed within the general population, a marked contrast to the Black–White segregation in most large American cities.

Unlike inner-city immigrants of the past, who tended to be socially concentrated, isolated, and economically disadvantaged, there is no longer a clear relationship between concentration and deprivation. Segregation, in and of itself, tells us little: some groups with a high degree of concentration, such as Jewish-Canadians, have high levels of educational attainment and income, while many dispersed groups do not. In Toronto, this latter group includes those with African and Afro-Caribbean ancestry, who are relatively dispersed throughout the city (Hiebert 1999; Myles and Hou 2003). Ultimately, residential patterns reflect a complex interaction of choice and constraint, and outcomes are conditional on the particularities of each group and their history.

Immigrant Suburban Neighborhoods

Despite the common conception of suburbs as a homogeneous landscape, in globalized cities they have become a hybrid of homogeneous and heterogeneous landscapes in terms of social class and ethnicity. The extent of this hybridization varies, but suburbs are becoming more heterogeneous, and in some cases even act as receiving areas for immigrants. As mentioned above, and as discussed in more detail in chapter 3, residential choice for many immigrants is based not on level of acculturation or socioeconomic necessity, but on the preferences of immigrants, such as living close to ethnic religious institutions and familiar cultural organizations. Increasingly, these preferences are best met in suburban communities. Also, affordable rental housing and extensive immigrant social institutions were once limited to the inner city, but these amenities, along with employment, are becoming increasingly available in the suburbs. The suburbanization of immigration over the past three decades has been dramatic. For example, in 1970, less than half of immigrants in Vancouver lived in suburbs, compared with three-quarters in 2010 (Statistics Canada 2013). Most recent new immigrants to Vancouver now move directly to the suburbs.

Scholars focusing on assimilation have traditionally conceived of suburbs as places where immigrants move after undergoing substantial cultural assimilation and economic mobility. However, current trends suggest that this notion is outdated. In fact, more intergroup separation is now being observed in the form of immigrant clustering in suburbs (Carter 2005). Due to the substantial ongoing immigration, this kind of residential ethnic concentration has increased recently in many multi-ethnic global cities.

Walks and Bourne (2006) suggested that the desire to live among similar others is particularly acute in complex multi-ethnic regions. However, closer examination of clusters of apparently homogeneous immigrant groups reveals heterogeneity along class and ethnic lines. For example, Lo and Wang (1997) found that Toronto immigrants of Chinese ethnicity living in the inner city differed from those living in the suburbs, with the former being less educated and having more precarious employment than the latter. Inner-city Chinese are more likely to be from mainland China or Vietnam, compared with suburban Chinese, who tend to obtain admittance to Canada as independent immigrants through their human capital and to originate from Hong Kong or Taiwan. Additionally, different suburbs tend to differ significantly in terms of birthplace sub-groups and arrival cohorts: immigrants arriving since 1984 have been more prone to suburban settlement (Statistics Canada 2013).

Conclusions

Residential patterns of immigrants are a major topic in understanding relations between immigrants and other groups in cities. These residential patterns both reflect and affect their social integration and potential interaction with other groups, and may also reflect the life chances and resources that immigrants may access.

Social scientists have long proposed models to explain the residential patterns of groups. In the early years, Burgess emphasized the role of economic attainment in achieving/increasing social integration: as their economic situation improves, immigrants move from the central city area, where co-ethnic neighborhoods are located and housing costs are low, to areas farther away from the central city. Firey, however, focused on the symbolic significance of neighborhoods and the co-ethnic social functions among neighbors that draw immigrants and their succeeding generations together.

Three important models have emerged recently that help explain immigrant residential patterns. Drawing from Burgess's arguments, the spatial assimilation model emphasizes the roles of socioeconomic resources and duration in the host country in reducing residential segregation among immigrants. The place stratification model explains why some groups may encounter difficulties moving into neighborhoods that have higher proportions of the majority group. Echoing Firey's work, such patterns occur because the locations are associated with status and prestige: the majority group does not want to share neighborhoods with disadvantaged groups, and tries to maintain the spatial hierarchy through various institutions. According to the group preference model, residential clustering may be related to the individual preference of living close to one's own group and/or the preference for a particular racial and ethnic composition in a neighborhood.

Research has yielded decidedly mixed findings that partially support all three perspectives. They clearly show the complexity of the residential patterns of groups, including immigrants from different racial and ethnic groups. Perhaps no single perspective can explain the varied findings. The clustering of different immigrant groups as observed in real cities likely reflects a variety of processes and combinations of various factors that have created a multi-layered reality. Researchers must sift through these complex patterns to identify the set of conditions and factors most likely to be operating. For example, newly arrived immigrants may be more likely to cluster together despite having financial resources. It may also be possible that some immigrants from groups that experience discrimination are more likely to cluster with their own group regardless of time in the host country.

In addition, the finding that growing numbers of neighborhoods have mixed racial and ethnic composition poses theoretical challenges. Some researchers have explored the effects of diverse racial and ethnic neighborhood composition on group relations, but most theoretical frameworks focus on majority–minority relations, and existing measures of segregation compare two groups. Therefore, the mixed neighborhood poses new challenges for researchers. For example, how is the segregation between two groups in a neighborhood affected by the presence of a third group or a combination of a third and fourth group? Research about residential patterns in a multi-group context will first require the challenging issue of how to theorize the combinations of various groups. Although multi-group segregation indexes have been devised to help scholars assess the level of segregation, theoretical understanding of how multiple groups interact and segregate is still limited.

Finally, the existence of gentrified neighborhoods, economically polarized immigrant neighborhoods, and immigrant suburban neighborhoods illustrate the complexity of the processes of immigrant adaptation and the relationships between immigrants and local residents. The existence of these neighborhoods challenges conventional wisdom about the positive relationship between the economic achievements of immigrants and their level of residential concentration. It also challenges researchers to better understand how local residents respond to these changes.

In short, most studies discussed here emphasized the need to rethink and re-evaluate the existing understanding of residential patterns among immigrants. They also call for a more comprehensive framework that is applicable across a diverse set of immigrant groups.

3

Housing Attainment, Homeownership, and the Immigrant Experience in Global Cities

The preceding chapter on residential patterns provided a broad overview of the classical and contemporary perspectives on segregation and preferences for integrated versus co-ethnic communities. This chapter focuses on how immigrants attain housing, often relying on their ethnic community or using particular strategies to progress in their housing "careers." Housing attainment pathways of immigrants are diverse, as are the community forms and economic organizations discussed in chapters 4 and 5.

Housing is shelter, but also a vital resource that provides or facilitates privacy, security, belonging, rootedness, neighborly social relations, status, and access to services. The housing "careers" of immigrants consist of the series of accommodations they have attained since migrating, often beginning with modest rental accommodation, but often leading to the widely aspired to goal of homeownership. Among immigrants and native-born people, homeownership is widely seen as a prudent investment, signaling commitment to a community. This chapter explores how housing attainment is an important part of the immigrant experience: it is instrumental in the process of adaptation to a new society, essential for security and sense of belonging, and visible through changes to the built form as immigrant cultures and tastes influence the housing landscape of cities. It focuses on questions such as: What are the housing careers of immigrants? How do their housing preferences and tastes reshape cities?

Just as there is no "average" immigrant, the housing experiences of immigrants are also varied. Immigrant entry classification (e.g., refugee, family, business/economic), socioeconomic status, language fluency, acculturation, and the relative characteristics of the origin country (e.g. GDP, cultural similarity) all contribute to the housing success and challenges of immigrants.

Immigrants tend to settle in a few "gateway" city-regions, and then cluster in specific areas within those regions. This has important consequences for their housing careers: gateway cities are generally more expensive than smaller cities and towns, making renting and ownership major barriers for many newcomers. However, the most significant divide in affordability is central city versus suburbs, with low-rent areas being much more common in cities than in the suburbs; this is especially the case in the United States. Ethnically concentrated neighborhoods can help immigrants attain housing: ethnic networks and shared language aid information-sharing and ethnic-linked housing supply. Some ethnic communities offer financial support, making proficiency in the host country's official language(s) less important when seeking suitable housing. Despite the short-term benefit of ethnically concentrated neighborhoods, for most immigrants, eventual assimilation and integration into the receiving society is associated with more positive long-term housing outcomes. However, this is not always the case: some immigrant groups such as the Chinese have been able to achieve economic integration and markers of success like homeownership without needing cultural or spatial assimilation, preferring to live in ethnic communities (Logan et al. 2002).

Scholars have sought to understand how cultural preferences and ethnic strategies operate to influence housing behavior. Conventional perspectives put most weight on the socioeconomic constraints of immigrant groups, suggesting that individual households will leave ethnic communities and integrate into mainstream society once they achieve economic success. However, closer examination reveals that group-level strategies rather than individual ones are often carried out in a rational and systematic way (e.g. savings clubs) to aid the housing attainment of group members. The degree of success and particular practices vary widely depending on the cultural backgrounds and internal dynamics of immigrant groups.

Global cities are increasingly being shaped by the housing decisions of immigrants. Immigrants may have more tolerance and familiarity with more compact housing and may even prefer it. This is affecting the demand for housing that accommodates larger households. Housing stock is changing to meet these demands, as seen in trends like the growth of high-rise living and multi-family housing. Ethnic tastes seen in the design and modification of the built form reflect the multicultural identity of immigrants, and also trickle back to affect mainstream visual culture. The look and feel of any city's housing stock is a reflection of its history and the cumulative multi-ethnic influences of immigrants.

Homeownership can be a significant marker of success and economic integration. It reflects an immigrant's attachment to the receiving society, and also facilitates further social integration and assimilation. The social benefits of homeownership for immigrants and non-immigrants alike are well documented: greater housing satisfaction, community involvement, civic participation, etc. However, there is still a homeownership gap between immigrant and native-born populations; the presence and size of this gap vary widely across ethnic groups based on factors such as the changing backgrounds and socioeconomic compositions of immigrants, as well as discrimination.

Diverse Immigrant Housing Experiences

Immigrants are more heterogeneous than in the past: there is no such thing as an "average" immigrant (Ley and Smith 2000). Housing outcomes vary by ethnicity as well as by immigrant classification. A study of immigrant housing in Toronto identified three classes: successful homeowners, financially precarious homeowners, and vulnerable renters (Preston et al. 2007). Mendez and colleagues (2006) found that in Canada, immigration classification is correlated with housing outcomes: "Business Class" and "Other Economic Class" arrivals can often draw on personal savings or family financial resources to quickly attain a foothold in homeownership. At the other end of the spectrum, immigrants classified as "Refugees" are much more likely to live in precarious and crowded housing conditions due to poverty and insufficient social or subsidized housing supply. Somewhere in the middle, "Family Class" arrivals have high levels of homeownership, but also have the highest likelihood of living in multiple-family dwellings.

New immigrants, along with visible minorities and the poor, are more likely to live in housing that is in disrepair, crowded relative to its size, and located in areas with higher crime rates and poorer access to job centers. In many cities, the supply of rental apartments suitable for immigrant families has not kept pace with the demand, resulting in higher rental rates and insufficient spaces for immigrants at the bottom of the income distribution. The issues of overcrowding and compact living will be examined in more detail later in this chapter. Despite the disadvantages faced by many immigrants, a sizable group of immigrants are more affluent than native-born residents, quickly becoming homeowners, and sometimes dramatically influencing market prices in some gateway cities like Vancouver, British Columbia.

What factors are responsible for shaping the diverse housing trajectories of immigrants? Many scholars have examined the determinants of immigrant housing and homeownership (Alba and Logan 1992; Borjas 2002; Coulson 1999; Krivo 1995; Myers and Lee 1998; Painter et al. 2004). Some have affirmed that immigrant homeownership is a symbol of integration/assimilation, demonstrating that acculturation is a key determinant in successful housing trajectories that end in homeownership. For example, in their study of 12 racial and ethnic groups in the United States, Alba and Logan (1992) found that immigrants who were more proficient in English were more likely to own homes. Similarly, in his analysis of the inequality between native-born Whites and Latino immigrants in the United States, Krivo (1995) found that being an immigrant is associated with worse household conditions, and that native immigrant traits or language use have aggregate effects that often undermine homeownership. Myers and Lee (1998) also demonstrated the importance of English-language proficiency in homeownership attainment in the United States.

Despite the success of particular groups, research conducted in both the United States and Canada suggests that immigrants, on average, have had declining homeownership rates since the 1980s relative to the native-born population (Borjas 2002). This trend may be linked to both socioeconomic and cultural factors. Recent immigration is predominantly from poorer emerging market Asian and Latin American countries, while mid-twentieth-century post-war immigrants were largely of European origin. However, sizable differences in homeownership rates remain by country of origin, even after adjusting for socioeconomic variables. Further insights into cultural norms and social activities from time-use data may help explain this. For example, Hamermesh and Trejo (2013) found that time use varies significantly among immigrants from different backgrounds: those from countries with a higher GDP are more likely than other immigrants to engage in assimilating activities on a given day. Recognizing the link between housing and assimilation, this may partly explain why immigrant home-ownership has been declining (Haan 2007) given the changing ethnic mix of immigrants – many of them now from developing countries with a low GDP.

Another factor that may hinder immigrant assimilation into a new society is discrimination in the housing market (Novac et al. 2002). Despite the rhetoric about inclusive housing, multiculturalism is not uniformly welcomed in the housing market. Both perceived and real discrimination are harmful to immigrants. Dion (2001) found that perceived housing discrimination toward immigrants in Canada is inversely proportional to satisfaction and successful incorporation into mainstream society. A number of studies conducted in Europe and North America have documented explicit discrimination in both the rental housing and home purchase markets. Ahmed and Hammarstedt (2008) found that applicants for rental housing in Sweden with Muslim/Arabic names were about half as likely to receive a response as those with a traditional Swedish name. In the United States, scholars have documented significant differences in access to rental housing by race and ethnicity (Carpusor and Loges 2006; Fischer and Massey 2004). Hogan and Berry's (2011) study of the increasingly important online rental housing market in Toronto revealed that Muslim/Arabic racialized men, followed by Southeast Asian men, and Black men and women, received fewer positive responses to rental inquiries. This differential treatment in the housing market leads to frustration and housing segregation by race and ethnicity.

Housing and Immigrant Clustering into Gateway Cities and Ethnic Neighborhoods

Characteristics of the cities chosen by immigrants also influence housing options and the gap in ownership compared to the native-born population (Borjas 2002). In the United States, one-third of immigrants live in just three city-regions (New York City, Los Angeles, and Miami). Geographic clustering of immigration in these large gateway city-regions, where homeownership rates are already relatively low, constrains housing choice. Coulson (1999) also traced lower levels of immigrant homeownership to gateway city-regions, which tend to have higher costs of homeownership.

Another important feature of geographic clustering of immigration in large city-regions is ethnically concentrated neighborhoods. Ethnic neighborhoods have long shaped the urban landscape of cities, and directly influence the housing careers of immigrants. Scholars have found both positive and negative effects of enclave residence. On one hand, ethnic clusters are conducive to establishing viable ethnic social networks. According to Toussaint-Comeau and Rhine, "such networks are likely to thrive in communities with ethnic businesses or banking and financial institutions with employees who speak the immigrants' language and who are familiar with their culture" (2000: 8). This can help immigrants navigate the housing market; for example, Toussaint-Comeau and Rhine found that English proficiency did not influence homeownership attainment in a Latino enclave in Chicago, a finding that contradicts earlier research (Alba and Logan 1992; Krivo 1995; Myers and Lee 1998). The increasing availability of ethnic lenders in some communities makes fluency in English less important for housing attainment than in the past. Similarly, Painter and colleagues (2004) found that English-language proficiency is becoming less necessary for homeownership attainment in the Chinese immigrant community in the United States and Canada. These findings also contradict previous research suggesting that immigrants who can speak multiple languages have a clear advantage.

Family and friendship networks are also important as immigrants settle into new housing. Ghosh (2007) examined the settlement of Indian Bengali and Bangladeshi immigrants in Toronto, and found that Bangladeshis, who relied on family and friendship ties to settle in an ethnic enclave, reported greater satisfaction with their initial settlement than Bengalis, who tended to rely on settlement agencies for their initial housing and therefore did not settle in neighborhoods with strong ethnic ties. This settlement experience went on to influence the later housing trajectories of the two groups, with Bangladeshis remaining concentrated in the ethnic neighborhoods and Bengalis dispersing into a much wider area over time.

Because of their relative success, contemporary Chinese immigrant communities have received much research attention. For Chinese immigrants, living in ethnic concentrations appears to be more positive in terms of attaining suitable housing and eventually homeownership than living among the general population (Painter et al. 2004). Residence in a Chinese immigrant community is also associated with homeownership rates that are even higher than those of the native-born population. These communities operate differently from traditional ethnically concentrated neighborhoods by making economic integration achievable without necessitating cultural or spatial assimilation (Logan et al. 2002), challenging the notion that homeownership is linked with assimilation. Fong and Chan (2010) found that Chinese immigrants are distinctive from other Asian immigrants in their use of co-ethnic real estate agents, further contributing to clustering beyond the sharing of other co-ethnic resources. Thus, the landscape of housing and immigration appears to be changing, at least for some groups. In today's immigrant communities, where residents share cultural preferences for homeownership and maintain a strong social network, living in these neighborhoods may bolster homeownership rates.

Despite research demonstrating benefits, immersion in an ethnic enclave may also hinder the prospects for better housing outcomes. A substantial body of literature emphasizes the importance of assimilation and acculturation for housing attainment (Alba and Logan 1992; Arbel et al. 2012; Constant et al. 2009; Krivo 1995; Myers and Lee 1998). A study of Latino neighborhoods in the United States found that ethnic residential clustering was associated with lower-quality housing and lower rates of homeownership than residence outside an enclave (Krivo 1995). One important reason for this may be that many Latino communities are clustered in part because of external hostility, racism, and economic disadvantage; these forces maintaining the enclave are quite different from the relative self-determination possible in some Chinese immigrant communities. Mexican cultural norms for larger families may also contribute to the increased crowding observed by Krivo in the enclaves.

Another disadvantage is that ethnic neighborhoods may no longer offer new immigrants the low-cost housing that was available in the past. Because many ethnic neighborhoods are concentrated in gateway cities where housing is expensive downtown and in the suburbs, affordability is becoming an important issue (Borjas 2002; Coulson 1999). Many recent low-income immigrants rely on these inner-city ethnic communities, many of which have been experiencing gentrification and diminished low-cost rental housing. Unfortunately, the increasing tendency for many immigrants to move directly to the suburbs does not mitigate housing affordability because suburban communities usually lack affordable housing choices due to "up-zoning" of suburban land use to favor expensive single-family homes (Li 1998b). Saiz (2007) found that increases in rental rates and housing cost are particularly acute in gateway city-regions with high immigration levels.

Overall, research is revealing shifts in terms of the nature of ethnically concentrated neighborhoods and their role in housing attainment and integration. These shifts vary by immigrant group, central city versus suburban location, and the time frame of evaluation (e.g., short- versus long-term consequences), among other variables. The short-term outcomes of living in an ethnic enclave are often positive, with ethnic social networks providing information and opportunities for securing jobs and housing, and sometimes offering living space (e.g., "doubling up") to address affordability problems. Cultural familiarity also helps mitigate barriers related to language issues or being uninformed about housing. Some, but not all, ethnic communities have the capacity to aid new immigrants with loans for home purchases. Despite the short-term benefits of ethnic clustering, the long-term benefits of eventual assimilation into a receiving society have been well established.

Immigrant Cultural Preferences, Group Strategies, and Housing Attainment

According to the spatial assimilation model, which was developed based on observations in the United States, ethnically concentrated neighborhoods serve as stepping-stones in the process of integration, with socioeconomic constraints necessitating initial settlement in these communities. However, as discussed in the previous chapter, recent immigrant settlement patterns are challenging this traditional model: many immigrants prefer to live in ethnic communities even after financial success (Logan et al. 2002). Research emphasis has shifted to explore how cultural preferences shape the housing adaptation process and outcomes of immigrant groups. As Søholt commented, "explanations have shifted from a focus on immigrants as victims of structures to ethnic networks, individual resources and immigrants as agents in their own lives" (2014: 1638). However, it is important to keep in mind that immigrant groups vary in the extent to which structures of inequality, racism, and discrimination serve as barriers to housing attainment, and some groups may have limited agency and self-determination. One limitation of this new focus on cultural preferences is that to date most studies have relied primarily on small case studies of particular ethnic groups, and few systematic quantitative analyses have been conducted.

Cultural preferences play an important role in the adaptive process in housing attainment, and recent work has revealed how immigrant groups navigate housing markets in culturally specific ways. For example, Søholt (2014) examined how Pakistani, Tamil, and Somali immigrants navigated the housing market in Oslo, Norway, revealing differences traceable to the cultural resources and internal dynamics of these groups. Pakistanis took an organized and pragmatic economic approach to group housing attainment that was fostered by cultural traditions of mutual trust and co-responsibility. Their housing trajectories were largely successful because members diligently participated in "saving clubs" in tight networks of family and close friends, where the group's fixed monthly contributions are distributed to a delegated participant to aid in home-buying costs. Like Pakistanis, Tamil immigrants were also organized and pragmatic in their housing strategy, systematically choosing settlement locations based on labor opportunities (Søholt 2014). Their strategy was to reduce housing costs and increase access by carefully meeting criteria and leveraging that access in the rental market. Expenses were also reduced by utilizing student housing, subletting provisions, and accommodation tied to working in particular industries (e.g., oil and gas). After achieving an economic foothold in the new society, Tamils shifted to a more active strategy that prioritized housing security, forming housing cooperatives, and seeking traditional homeownership.

Unlike Pakistanis and Tamils, Somali immigrants in Oslo experienced more difficulties in finding suitable housing, and achieved much lower long-term rates of homeownership (Søholt 2014). They were initially set back by inexperience with bureaucratic systems that emphasize written communication, hindering their ability to navigate rules and leverage housing opportunities. Nomadic cultural traditions in part emphasize spontaneous problem-solving efforts that can solve short-term housing problems, but do not yield coherent long-term strategies for positive housing outcomes. For example, many Somalis in Oslo dealt with housing shortage by temporarily hosting other Somalis as guests; although these spontaneous acts of generosity prevented families from being homeless, they did not represent the rational planning that is necessary for sustained and long-term progress in the housing market. Mensah and Williams (2014) also noted that because interest on loans is religiously prohibited for Somalis, they face greater impediments in their housing acquisition than other groups.

Immigrant Crowding and Compact Living: Tolerance or Preference?

Since the Industrial Revolution, urban sociologists and housing policymakers have been preoccupied with overcrowding in cities. However, the definition of "crowded" is subjective, varying over time and by group. Cultural preferences, or at least tolerance, for dense living conditions are clearly visible in the adaptive housing strategies of some immigrant groups. Carter (2005) found that immigrants in Toronto were more willing than native-born residents to tolerate and resort to crowding, doubling up and sometimes having two or more families within a household, and experiencing high levels of "core housing need." Similarly, Bae (2004) found that recent immigrants to the United States and Canada were more accustomed to living in high-density living environments, leading to increasing demand for high-rise apartments and condominium living. Bae observed crowded and multi-family households in both owned and rented housing, with household members sharing a common goal of increasing affordability and saving money. These practices sometimes come into conflict with local norms and standards about household size and composition, bringing allegations of unsafe overcrowding or unfair use of public services relative to property taxes paid.

Myers (2001) argued that Latinos in the United States, especially foreign-born, have cultural traits independent of economic circumstances: they can tolerate dense living conditions and tend to favor compact city lifestyles. Myers found that Latinos tended to have larger mean household sizes, and to engage in more multi-family housing, more apartment living, and more commuting on foot, by bike, or public transit than the general population, after controlling for income. However, preference for compact living may not be a Latino trait, but may rather be an immigrant trait, because other scholars have found that native-born Latinos tend to have lower rates of crowding than Anglos, after adjusting for socioeconomic status (Krivo 1995).

Time-use data provide some further and perhaps contradictory insights into the trade-offs immigrants make in choosing housing in compact central communities versus more spacious housing further from city centers. For example, immigrants tend to have longer commuting times compared to native-born individuals (Preston et al. 1998). Further work is needed to elaborate on what this finding reveals about immigrant housing choice, but it may reflect shifting cultural preferences about housing among immigrants, or simply that housing choices are as heterogeneous as today's immigrants, who in some cases trade commuting burden for space and affordability.

Although many immigrants lived communally in large households before they migrated, crowding observed among immigrants in their new host country may reflect both economic constraints as well as preferences. Crowding in a new country can be driven as much by economic necessity as a desire to live together. Mensah and Williams (2014) explored the interplay between culture and housing in interviews with Somali and Ghanaian immigrants in Toronto. They found that communal housing arrangements are common and even desired in Africa, but in the context of Toronto, overcrowding is perceived as a burden because financial constraints and money-saving strategies dictate housing choice. The apartments and homes in North American cities are also less likely to be designed for larger multi-family households. The Toronto study noted how housing predominantly intended for nuclear family arrangements did not fit well with the cultural preferences of the immigrant families studied, who desire extended family living arrangements or gender-specific room allocations.

This inconsistency between housing size and desired living arrangements of immigrants is not new or confined to any particular city. In some cases, housing designed for nuclear families has thwarted extended families from living together. In other cases, families have doubled up and tripled up with multiple generations and families living within one house or apartment. Extended family residences have been the norm for centuries in North America. For example, in New York City, large families occupied single tenements in the city's Lower East Side. Both past and present, two- and three-family houses are found in many Canadian and US cities of all sizes.

Housing Modifications that Embody Immigrant Cultural Values

Not surprisingly, immigrants go on to reshape housing in a way consistent with their household practices and cultural traditions. These values and preferences become embodied in the physical design and modification of housing. Several studies have focused on modifications to Italian immigrant homes, the reasons for the changes, and how they leave an ethnic imprint on neighborhoods and the urban landscape (Buzzelli, 2001; Harney, 2006; Pascali, 2006). For example, Pascali (2006) investigated the popularity of basement kitchens in many first-generation Italian homes in Canada and the United States. While basement kitchens are relatively unknown in Italy, in North America they appear to act as liberating spaces, free from the constraints of formality and room divisions of traditional homes; upstairs kitchens are changed into showpieces to be kept in pristine condition for guests.

Agrawal (2006) examined how Indian homes in Toronto are renovated to embody the cultural and aesthetic values of Indian culture. However, these modifications are primarily internal and utilitarian, emphasizing open space and geometric symmetry consistent with Indian artistic traditions. They contrast with the extensive exterior modifications more common among homes of southern Europeans like Portuguese, Greeks, or Italians, which express ethnic values with brick arches, grillwork rails, angle-brick facades, and statues and figurines on their lawns. Intensive knowledge and involvement in construction and masonry among Portuguese and Italians likely aided the expression of cultural preferences through extensive exterior work.

Cultural preferences of some immigrants for new and modern aesthetics, or at least indifference to many of the European-inspired architectural forms common in North America and Europe, also shape the housing landscape. For example, many Asian immigrants eschew traditional Victorian-inspired brick homes for spacious newly constructed homes that are more common in suburban locations. These preferences in part may explain the suburbanization of immigrant communities. Another example is that many new high-rise condominium developments and units are explicitly designed and positioned following Chinese feng shui practices and avoidance of unlucky numbers. The importance of water views among some Asian immigrant housing investors has played a role in creating demand for the redevelopment of disused waterfronts, contributing to high-rise condominium building booms in cities like Toronto and Vancouver.

Immigrants and Homeownership

Homeownership is an important focus of research because it is linked to many positive effects related to the long-term commitment and social stability it provides to occupants. Dietz and Haurin (2004) found that homeowners have higher levels of community involvement, voting rates, child educational returns, life satisfaction, self-esteem, and neighborhood connectedness. These positive findings apply to both immigrant and non-immigrant populations. Simone and Newbold (2014) examined data from the Longitudinal Survey of Immigrants to Canada (LSIC: 2001–2005), and found that housing tenure is the single most influential variable for satisfaction because the 'Canadian dream' of homeownership provides a deep sense of security. Arbel and colleagues (2012) found that civic participation is significantly higher among immigrant homeowners than non-owners in Israel.

Homeownership is a visible indicator of achievement in an

immigrant's housing career, often perceived as representing socioeconomic attainment and economic integration (Alba and Logan 1992; Borjas 2002; Kim and Boyd 2009; Myers and Lee 1998). In some ways, it is a better measure of long-term integration of immigrants than income or education, because it requires a substantial financial and social investment and signals commitment to a particular location (Sinning 2010).

The relationship between homeownership and attachment to a receiving society is mutually reinforcing: high levels of attachment can foster the desire to be a homeowner, and owning a home can foster further attachment through the psychological effects of ownership as well as the opportunities and stability present in homeowner communities. Conversely, lack of attachment to a new society can weaken the desire to be a homeowner, preventing access to stable housing situations that tend to promote a sense of security and connection. Several scholars have investigated this relationship in immigrant communities. Constant and colleagues (2009) investigated how the ethnic identity of immigrants in Germany – measured as attachment to Germany versus their country of origin – shaped their housing attainment. Immigrants with a stronger attachment to German culture, regardless of attachment to their origin country, had higher rates of homeownership. Similarly, Arbel and colleagues (2012) investigated immigrant homeownership in Israel, and found that respect for Israel was positively correlated with owning a home.

Owusu (1998) found that a lack of attachment to the receiving society limits the housing careers of immigrants; specifically, that the low homeownership rate among Ghanaians in Toronto could be explained by their desire to return home and invest in Ghana. Similarly, Søholt (2014) found that Pakistani immigrants in Oslo were influenced by a "myth of returning to Pakistan" that delayed their housing careers.

Several studies have reported that the length of time an immigrant has spent in the new country increases the likelihood of homeownership (Kim and Boyd 2009; Myers and Lee 1998). This is partly due to economic successes over time, but it also reflects that fact that attachment increases with time. Individuals who do not form an attachment to the receiving society are more likely to leave through out-migration. Thus, positive housing outcomes, such as homeownership, can be both a cause and a consequence of a higher level of commitment to the receiving society. However, the relationship may vary depending on the peculiarities of a country's cultural orientation to homeownership and supports for immigrants. Interestingly, Sinning (2010) reported conflicting results: he found that the duration of residence in Germany did not affect the probability of homeownership among immigrants, suggesting that homeownership may play a less important role in the assimilation process in Germany. This finding may be partly explained by the fact that average German homeownership rates are much lower than those in North America; also, he argues that German immigration policy tends to focus on short-term rather than long-term economic effects, so immigrants may not feel incentivized to invest in housing.

If immigrant homeownership increases political participation and community involvement, then perhaps homeownership should be viewed as more than just a proxy for economic integration; it could also be viewed as a contributing to social integration.[1] One possible mechanism for this is the effects of economic pressures of homeownership, which could encourage immigrants to behave in ways similar to native-born homeowners. For example, time-use research has revealed that immigrant women tend to spend more time doing housework and less time on market work compared with their native-born counterparts (Ribar 2012; van Klaveren et al. 2011; Zaiceva and Zimmermann 2014). This reflects traditional cultural norms among many immigrants, whereby men assume the role of breadwinners while women handle the domestic responsibilities. This gender division of labor is one reason why it takes immigrants longer to purchase homes after marriage (Magnusson Turner and Hedmen 2014). Homeownership and housing debts can encourage women to enter the labor market (Fortin 1995; Joesch, 1994). Additionally, engaging in paid work outside the home may increase their contact with native-born residents and provide then with integrative experiences.

The Immigrant Homeownership Gap: Causes and Consequences

A large body of literature has documented a significant homeownership gap between native-born and immigrant groups. Immigrants (and minorities in general) in many advanced industrialized countries (e.g., United States, Canada, Israel and in Europe) have lower rates of homeownership than native-born residents even after controlling for socioeconomic status (Alba and Logan 1992; Arbel et al. 2012; Borjas 2002; Coulson 1999; Haan 2007; Krivo 1995; Myers and Lee 1998; Sinning 2010). However, the disadvantage to immigrants does not apply to all cases, and generally decreases with time in the country. Bourassa (1994) conducted a study in Australia and found that on average, immigrants and native-born individuals are no different in housing tenure, and some immigrant groups are more likely than the native-born population to be homeowners. Similarly, Laryea (1999) found that immigrants in Canada achieve higher rates of homeownership than native-born Canadians within ten years of arrival (61 percent of immigrants versus 54 percent of native-born Canadians).

Despite these findings, more recent immigrants to the United States and Canada have not matched the homeownership success of past generations (Laryea 1999; Sinning 2010). Homeownership was very high among post-World War II immigrants, especially those coming from southern Europe, but immigrant homeownership rates declined between 1971 and 2006 (Preston et al. 2007). Haan (2007) compared immigrant homeownership rates in the United States and Canada, and found strong similarities between the two countries, including recent increases in the gap between native-born and immigrant homeownership rates. As of 2001, Canadian immigrants who arrived between 1965 and 1969 had an 8 percent higher homeownership advantage in 1981, but this advantage reversed to a 7 percent disadvantage for the 1985–9 cohort. Haan (2007) also found that homeownership rates varied considerably in both countries according to ethnic background, with Whites and Chinese in both Canada and the United States having much higher levels. This hierarchy by ethnicity was not observed in other housing attainment measures.

Conclusions

This review of research about immigrants' housing attainment and homeownership in global cities revealed that pathways of housing attainment are as diverse as immigrants themselves. Housing outcomes may be affected by individual, family, or multiple contextual factors. Individual and family-level factors such as socioeconomic resources, cultural familiarity of a host society, and official language fluency can hinder or facilitate access to information, housing opportunities, and mortgages. Contextual factors such as housing costs, housing supply, and the presence of family and co-ethnic networks and ethnic neighborhoods within the gateway city will also influence housing attainment. Country and international-level factors may also be important: immigration policy can increase or reduce the number of newcomers vying for housing, and outlays for social housing offered to immigrants and refugees can also make a big difference in housing attainment.

Ethnically concentrated neighborhoods remain important sources of housing help for new arrivals, but most research suggests that long-term housing attainment prospects are better when immigrants assimilate into the wider society. However, a newer body of scholarship shows that acculturation and social integration are not required for some immigrants, who achieve high levels of homeownership and economic integration while remaining in ethnic communities. The nature of ethnic neighborhoods is changing as well: some immigrants have created new suburban auto-centric enclaves with high levels of homeownership. Whether homes are located in a new suburban or traditional central-city ethnic neighborhood, group cultural norms and practices are key to the housing success of members; they shape practices around co-ethnic cooperation in housing attainment, as well as preferences for clustered living, multi-family households, and tolerance for crowding.

Despite the housing successes of many immigrants, immigrants face considerable disadvantage in the housing market. First, at the bottom of the housing market, many immigrants face challenges securing and retaining quality rental housing. Gentrification and the lack of affordable housing development in many gateway cities have resulted in many immigrant families spending a large fraction of their income on rent, or crowding into apartments that are not suitable for their households. Challenges like these make it difficult for many immigrants to get on the path to homeownership, the widely cherished goal sought by immigrants and native-born residents alike. These local housing market challenges, and the fact that many recent immigrants arrive from poorer countries, have resulted in an increasing homeownership gap between immigrant and native-born populations in North America since the 1970s. Furthermore, homeownership is a bigger challenge than in past generations because the affordability ratio of first-time buyers has declined from 1 in 2 in the 1950s to about 1 in 15 today, regardless of birthplace. Discrimination in the housing market, both perceived and documented, also limits where immigrants can live. Together, these barriers tend to weaken the attachment of immigrants to the receiving society. Ideally, pro-immigration public policy should actively seek to enhance housing supply and availability, encouraging a positive cycle whereby suitable housing nurtures attachment and attempts to integrate.

Despite the challenges discussed above, many immigrants eventually have successful housing careers and reach important goals like homeownership. Case studies have revealed that immigrants may take a variety of different paths to reach their goals: group cultural norms and preferences yield unique adaptive strategies that help immigrants navigate the housing market in ways that match their strengths and perspectives. Homeownership is an especially important outcome for many immigrants, because owning a home provides stability and social opportunities for all members of the family by making a locational commitment that fosters further assimilation and acculturation. Indeed, homeownership may hold a greater significance, or at least a different kind of significance, for immigrants than for native-born individuals because it represents a secure foothold after a long and uncertain journey of migration.

4

Immigration and Ethnic Community

In addition to occupying the same residential areas as described in chapter 2, immigrants cluster and form their own communities. Scholars have offered various definitions of "neighborhood" and "community" (Delmelle 2015; Galster 2001). Here, "immigrant neighborhood" refers to the geographic clustering of immigrants, usually along racial and ethnic lines, within a few residential blocks, while "immigrant community" refers to the constellation of social relations and activities supported by ethnic co-organizations with or without geographic concentration. In an immigrant community, social relations emerge between immigrants and between immigrants and the organizations in which they are involved. These relationships usually fall along racial and ethnic lines; they bind members together and give them a sense of belonging and shared identity. Social ties include "strong ties," such as between family and close friends, and "weak ties," which emerge when getting to know others in settings like ethnic churches, organizations, or events (Putnam 2000). These social relations are forged, nurtured, and reinforced through participation in ethnic organizations. Participants are motivated to form ties and develop new organizations because they share similar immigrant experiences, cultural practices, expectations, and social concerns. Geographic proximity is important but not essential for facilitating these social relations. For example, the Internet has made it easier to communicate and share information, allowing immigrant communities to maintain social relations within broader geographic boundaries.

Therefore, it might be most appropriate to view immigrant communities as primarily being defined by symbolic boundaries that are maintained through the social ties between individuals and organizations in the community. These boundaries function to distinguish "us" versus "them" in the collective minds of members (Wimmer 2008).

Immigrant communities are commonly found in major immigrant destination cities (Singer 2008). Although some are still located in older urbanized parts of these cities, many of the largest and fastest growing immigrant communities are now found in suburban municipalities (Fong et al. 2015; Hall 2013; Hin and Xin 2011; Wang et al. 2009). These suburban immigrant communities often include co-ethnic restaurants, non-governmental organizations, and after-school classes. The level of concentration varies by group: some immigrant communities may just have a few co-ethnic shops clustered on a street, and many more co-ethnic organizations and businesses scattered throughout the city. Other immigrant groups may have developed a high concentration of organizations within a small geographic territory, representing a more traditional model of institutional completeness. Despite the variations in geographic concentration, members of immigrant communities maintain a high level of social closeness with one another through routine activities that nurture social ties.

Immigrant communities, in all their various forms, are an integral part of the social and economic life of immigrants. They have strong effects on the adaptation process and outcomes of immigrants. This chapter explores the reasons for the emergence of immigrant communities and the nature of these communities. It also presents two recent developments in immigrant communities: the "ethnoburb" (Li 1998b); and the integral role of transnational activities within immigrant communities (Portes et al. 2007). These suburban shifts and global connections illustrate how the activities of immigrant communities and their locations have become more diverse and dispersed. These shifts add to the vibrancy and growth of the community by raising the life chances of immigrants and their children, making contemporary immigrant communities appealing destinations for other immigrants.

Emergence of the Immigrant Community

Immigrant communities emerge when immigrants cluster in the same place. The clustering process is partly related to the process of chain migration: migrants follow their friends, relatives, or fellow villagers to a particular place, where they can more easily obtain support and information. As immigrants cluster, they form their own parallel social organizations, such as ethnic churches, schools, and even banks. These institutions help recent immigrants adjust to the new environment though more familiar social relations. Thomas and Znaniecki (1995) were among the first to explore the organization of an immigrant community, specifically Polish peasants in the United States. They argued that initially, waves of immigration weakened the organization of the existing Polish-American community, to the point that it was not able to build or improve social relations. In the face of so many new Polish immigrants, the existing community needed to adjust its values and attitudes to create stability. As Persons (1987) succinctly summarized Thomas and Znaniecki's idea, the immigrant "on arrival joined a society of his own people, and the character of that society was the principal influence in determining the desire and capacity of the immigrant to participate in American life. The function of these societies was not to Americanize, but to give life its necessary continuity. They permitted the immigrant to take the first step in the transition from one cultural world to another" (Persons 1987: 55).

In another classic work, *The Ghetto*, Wirth (1962) provided a detailed account of the settlement of immigrant Jews. They tended to cluster in areas with low rent, so most properties needed repair, and living conditions were rudimentary and crowded. Despite these poor housing conditions, a key asset of the "ghetto" was the shared cultural characteristics on which community organizations could be based. Most organizations in the community were based on Jewish traditions commonly found in Jewish communities in large European cities. Social ties in the ghetto were so close that the Jewish social world was almost an enclosure. Breton (1964) described the Jewish community in Montreal as "institutionally complete," meaning that it provided virtually all the social and economic activities that individuals required to conduct their daily lives, which they continued to live as they had in Europe. However, Wirth also believed that the ghetto boundaries would quickly blur, and that the younger generation would adopt an American way of life and move out of the ghetto.

Most early studies of immigrant communities suggested that two important processes are involved in the emergence of ethnic community. First, the social relations and activities within an immigrant community are strongly influenced by the experiences of its members before immigration. An immigrant community can be viewed as a continuation of social life before immigration; it provides a familiar cultural environment as immigrants settle in the new country. For example, restaurants or businesses in immigrant communities are often named after major landmarks, cities, or streets "back home," and social organizations closely follow the structures and operational procedures that were used in their home country. Second, the ethnic community helps immigrants adjust to the new society. For example, social support from co-ethnic members can considerably reduce the social, psychological, and economic costs to immigrants.

Changes in immigration policies in the early 1970s in Canada and the United States have led to increases in numbers of middle-class immigrants with post-secondary education and professional training (Zhou 1997). Recent studies suggest that immigrant communities do not emerge only from poor areas; potential immigrants with assets are increasingly being welcomed and encouraged to relocate by governments seeking foreign investment (Li 1998b; Zhou 1997). In some cases, real estate agents facilitate these moves by offering real estate investments (Fong and Chan 2010; Horton 1995; Po 2011). This is partly the result of the ease in transferring money across international borders. Some real estate developers have enjoyed healthy profits by targeting immigrants and potential immigrants with financial resources to new middle-class developments, which become immigrant communities. Cities including Toronto and Vancouver have benefitted from a steady flow of educated middle-class immigrants contributing to the tax base and real estate development (Ley 2010).

Horton (1995) focused on Monterey Park, California, and found that Chinese immigrants first began to settle in this middle-class suburban community in the 1970s. Today, the community is full of Chinese supermarkets, pharmacies, medical clinics, and restaurants. Chinese have a long history in California, partly because the climate is close to that of their home country. Real estate developers have also played an important role in promoting Monterey Park as the "Chinese Beverly Hills" to attract middle-class immigrants from Taiwan and Hong Kong.

Other studies have consistently shown that ethnic real estate brokers steer their co-ethnic members to certain communities. In the early 1980s, South Asians began to concentrate in Edison, a middle-class suburb in New Jersey, after a real estate developer promoted it as a "piece of the American Dream" (Light 2006: 117). Teixeira (2007) documented how Portuguese immigrants were steered by co-ethnic real estate agents during their housing search, which contributed to the development of Portuguese communities in Mississauga, Canada. Fong and Chan (2010) reported similar findings among Chinese immigrants in Toronto, where high concentrations of Chinese immigrants are largely associated with use of co-ethnic real estate agents.

The changing socioeconomic background of immigrants has led to a variety of immigrant communities. As discussed above, it is not uncommon for middle-class immigrants to be targeted in the promotion of specific communities. Zhou (1997) explored how today's immigrant communities have varying socioeconomic resources, which can be traced to varying socioeconomic resources upon arrival. For example, changes in the economy and labor markets in Western nations beginning in the 1970s reduced the need for low-skill and low-education workers and increased the need for highly educated workers (Zhao and Webster 2011). Manufacturing has rapidly declined, while financial services have become more important to the overall economy. Now, immigrants with low levels of education and skill in major immigrant-receiving countries like the United States, Canada, and Australia find that their job opportunities and wages are dismal. As a result, the economic gap has widened between those with higher levels of education and skill and those with lower levels of education and skill. Immigrant communities have similarly become stratified based on this socioeconomic gap (Zhou 1997).

Whether immigrant communities with diverse socioeconomic resources emerge from a natural process of differentiation or from the actions of real estate developers, there is variation in how residents in these different communities integrate. One reason for this is the varying resources available to different immigrant communities. When leaders of immigrant communities have a higher level of education and better language skills, they are more capable of gaining strategic access and resources for their community, thus ensuring more formal and informal organizations able to provide better support services.

In short, the development of immigrant communities has moved from a natural ecological outcome of immigrant clustering to a combination of the consequences of promotions by real estate developers and the natural preference of immigrants to cluster. With immigrants coming from different socioeconomic backgrounds, the changing understanding of the development of immigrant communities in recent decades reflects the recognition that an immigrant community may be developed as an opportunity created to obtain revenue, rather than simply a natural and inevitable process of adaptation in response to immigrant demand.

Functions of Immigrant Communities

Immigrant communities provide various types of social support to immigrants and their children. This section presents a few types of these social supports, which may vary by socioeconomic background or gender of immigrants.

Immigrant communities are a crucial venue for providing a wide array of social support to immigrants when they arrive in the host country (Burgess 1925; Logan and Alba 1999). These supports can be obtained through informal social ties developed in the immigrant community; they can also be obtained through formal participation in community organizations (Wu and Hu 2011). The informal social support provided by co-ethnic friends and relatives ranges from minor help like filling in legal papers to major assistance such as lending money.

Organizations, ranging from soccer clubs to language classes, play an important role in developing and maintaining immigrant networks and accessing a variety of information, from elections to jobs (Small 2002). These supports help lower the cost of integration and reduce the stress of facing an unfamiliar social environment. Small (2009) argued that meeting friends in community centers yields "unanticipated gains." For example, single mothers may significantly reduce stress by meeting friends and developing friendships there. Massey and his colleagues (1990) developed a theory of cumulative causation of immigration, arguing that a larger immigrant community can offer more and diverse supports, and thereby reduce the social, economic, and psychological costs of integration. Through social ties and support from the community, immigrants learn over time how to access public services in the new society, such as education and health care. They gradually connect to the larger society, while maintaining ties with their own group.

Immigrant communities also provide a social network and a safe environment where immigrants can share grievances. In a supportive social environment where open discussion is encouraged by community leaders, grievances can be translated and marshaled into mobilized collective action. Olzak (1992) even suggested that sharing grievances within the immigrant community is one of the key factors associated with an increase in the likelihood of ethnic conflict. Other scholars have since made similar arguments that contextual conditions shape the level of individual grievances, which can in turn foster group conflict (Bach 2010; Liu et al. 2010a). Others have noted that the community context helps provide organizational support and framing for mobilization (Benford and Snow 2000; Okamoto 2003).

However, participating in immigrant community organizations does not necessarily increase mobilization. In her study of immigrant participation in labor unions, Terriquez (2011) found that immigrants participating in activities that involve decision-making, advocacy, and enhanced organizational skills are more likely to promote further mobilization. Thus, it is not simply membership in the community organizations that enhances mobilization, but the nature and extent of activity in them. In his detailed analysis of the governance of ethnic communities, Breton (1991) also stressed that leaders with higher education, better language ability, and more economic resources are more successful in mobilizing their co-ethnic immigrants and help them acquire better skills and more knowledge to understand the situation and negotiate with individuals outside the group.

Children also can benefit from vibrant and active immigrant communities. Zhou and Bankston (1998) focused on Vietnamese refugees in Louisiana, and found that community organizations provided services to help immigrant children adapt to the American educational system and learn about the expectations of the system. This kind of assistance is particularly obvious in Asian immigrant communities. Lee and Zhou (2014) argued that the strong performance of Asian immigrants reflects the high education and professional skills of their parents, who brought a "success frame" with them to the new country. This success frame encourages strong investment in their children's education and support of community activities to promote learning, such as after-class tutoring.

As well as providing practical after-school tutoring, these institutions tend to serve as a buffer between immigrant networks and the wider society. They help to maintain social control over younger members by socializing them with traditional value systems to retain connections with their parents and the goal of upward mobility (Zhou and Bankston 1998). As they share similar values and norms, consensus becomes the basis of effective social control. Overall, integrating children into immigrant communities allows them to adopt the positive aspects of the host society, while shielding them from influences seen as negative.

Immigrant communities also provide job opportunities, either directly or indirectly, through information exchange (Portes and

Bach 1985; Wilson and Portes 1980). Information exchange is valuable because it may offer new business ideas or link potential investors with prospective entrepreneurs. In fact, immigrant entrepreneurship is now considered a major engine for economic growth (Light and Gold 2000). Chapter 5 will explore ethnic economy and businesses in depth. In this chapter, we discuss how immigrant entrepreneurship and business development benefit from immigrant community.

Immigrant communities benefit in three main ways from fostering immigrant businesses. First, the clustering of immigrants and co-ethnic members in the ethnic community ensures a supply of labor and demand for products and services (Light and Gold 2000). It has long been suggested that the size of a group is crucial in developing group activities (Fischer 1972). Studies of Chinatown show that the diversity of businesses in different industrial sectors grew as the population in the immigrant community increased (He et al. 2010). Second, the close co-ethnic network associated with the immigrant community can reduce operational costs (Yang and Wang 2007). Networks allow easy promotion of new products and sales, and easy and inexpensive recruitment of potential employees. Additionally, products may be obtained from co-ethnic wholesalers at bigger discount and on more favorable terms. Third, the immigrant community provides a co-ethnic network for distributing business information and facilitating employee recruitment. Immigrant networks in the community help to more quickly spread the news to potential customers in the community.

Men and women tend to use different resources in immigrant communities, and to derive different benefits (Fong et al. 2010). Given that most immigrants maintain traditional gender roles, males and females rely on different sets of information to adjust to the new environment. Males may require more information about the labor market, while females may seek information related to daily activities, such as grocery shopping. Males and females also differ in terms of mobilization in the community because they have different expectations. Males may be more concerned about conditions and benefits in the workplace, while females may care more about social programs for their children. Finally, jobs generated by ethnic businesses in the immigrant community may be more critical for males, as female immigrants may assume the traditional role of staying at home.

Negative Consequences of Immigrant Communities

Close ties among immigrants in the community foster ethnic solidarity and promote sharing of resources through community networks. However, because there is limited time available for interactions with others, more interactions within one's own group mean less time for those outside the group (Portes and Sensenbrenner 1993). Less interaction with other groups can lead to more separation from the rest of society, so although immigrant communities can provide many benefits to members, close-knit immigrant communities can also have negative effects on long-term integration. Data collected in Toronto reveal that individuals with close connections to immigrant communities are less likely to have friends outside their own group, after controlling for various social and demographic factors (Fong and Ooka 2002). Echoing these findings, members of ethnic networks with limited resources have less useful information about the job market than those in networks with more resources (Ooka and Wellman 2006). Some researchers have concluded that living in an immigrant community with limited resources can negatively affect the trajectories and outcomes of immigrant integration (Nee et al. 1994). In addition, a closed network in the immigrant community, with too much reliance on co-ethnic support, may sometimes have negative consequences because of conflicts of interest and nepotism (Portes and Sensenbrenner 1993). Decisions may not be in the best interest of members if outside advice or expertise cannot be recruited. A closed network may limit job opportunities to only co-ethnic members, who may not be the best available candidates. Closed networks also tend to involve strong obligations to hire friends or relatives, and may lead to a business becoming a sort of "welfare hotel" (Portes 2014).

Portes and Sensenbrenner (1993) explain that closed networks in immigrant communities may foster this excessive communitarianism through four mechanisms that link expected behavior with social capital. The first expectation is value introjection. Individuals are expected to behave in certain ways for the collectivity. They sometimes may be considered "oversocialized." In such context, individuals have to act for the benefit of the collectivity (the immigrant community or their family and friends) instead of for themselves. This may cause individual businesses or individual wellbeing to suffer. The second expectation is that the norm of reciprocity should govern transactions within the community. Individuals are expected to repay whatever they have been given, which may incur high costs and may be harmful to their social and economic wellbeing. For example, individual members are obliged to provide financial support to friends to help them get settled when they arrived in the country, even if the friends have limited resources and are not likely to pay them back. The third expectation is bounded solidarity. A clear and enclosed group boundary encourages solidarity among members. However, some individuals may take advantage of this group solidarity and become free riders, claiming entitlement to various benefits whether or not they meet the qualification criteria. The fourth expectation is enforceable trust. Trust among members is enforced through community institutions, and tangible and intangible rewards and punishments are used to maintain this trust. However, an enforceable environment can limit individual expression, creative ideas, and extension of networks beyond one's own group. Additionally, powerful ethnic community associations may regulate resources and guaranteed privileges to co-ethnic business owners or other elites; they can also control the extent to which these business members could have actions and contacts outside the immigrant community.

In sum, immigrant communities provide many benefits to immigrants and their children, but these benefits come at a cost. Most studies focus on the advantages of immigrant communities, so more research is needed to explore this double-edged sword and the potential negative consequences for male and female immigrants and their children.

New Trends in Immigrant Communities

Emergence of the "Ethnoburb"

As mentioned in chapter 2, the residential settlement of immigrants has changed dramatically in recent decades. Suburbanization has affected many who live in metropolitan areas, and immigrants are no exception. Although the relative housing quality and affluence in the suburbs and downtown varies from city to city, many immigrants find the larger homes and auto-centric life of the suburbs to be appealing. Some newly arriving immigrants with economic resources choose to settle in suburbs right away due to the better housing and amenities. Other immigrants may initially settle in an ethnic community, and then move to the suburbs later after improving their socioeconomic resources. Some of these may cluster, seeding a new suburban immigrant community. Immigrant communities with economic and social activities emerged. Li (1998a; 1998b) called this new spatial pattern the "ethnoburb," writing:

> Ethnoburbs can be recognized as suburban ethnic clusters of residential areas and business districts in large metropolitan areas. The local context of the ethnoburb is characterized by both vibrant ethnic economies, due to the presence of large numbers of ethnic people, and strong ties to the globalizing economy, revealing their role as outposts in the emerging international economic system. Ethnoburbs are also multi-ethnic communities, in which one ethnic minority group has a significant concentration, but does not necessarily comprise a majority. (Li 1998a: 482)

According to Li, ethnoburbs have three unique characteristics. First, the ethnoburb has a unique economy with strong international linkages. Many residents have high levels of education, professional credentials, and knowledge of their home country, and many are involved in the global economy, in particular banking and trade. These international economic activities serve as a bridge between the home country and the host country, and allow many immigrants to travel between both places. Such characteristics are different from traditional immigrant communities, where economic activities emerge in response to immigrant adaptation.

Second, the ethnoburb consists of both commercial and residential businesses in a suburban area. In other words, local residents seek economic and social activities in the same area where they reside. Given the diverse socioeconomic backgrounds of people living in ethnoburbs, the services provided in different ethnoburbs are usually also diverse. Ethnoburbs are usually institutionally complete, so residents tend to have minimal interaction with people outside their own group, which may foster a certain level of social separation.

Third, most ethnoburbs are located in areas shared with other groups. However, this does not necessarily entail interaction between groups. As Fischer suggested in "Toward a Subcultural Theory of Urbanism" (1975), diversity fosters the development of subgroups. Suttles' (1968) classic study in Chicago showed that immigrant groups maintained clear territories even as they shared a community with other groups. Similar customs and culture and a strong sense of group identity encourage group interaction. With low density land use in suburbs, immigrant groups that share a suburban area can occupy separate locations for their activities without much interaction with one another. However, tension or conflict can emerge when activities are not confined to a group's own territory. Some of these conflicts may be a consequence of "the paradox of integration" (Oliver 2010) and may result from different ways of life or competition for resources. Horton's study (1995) of Monterey Park, a typical ethnoburb in Los Angeles, clearly documented how immigrants and minority groups organize themselves to compete for resources through the political process.

The Integral Role of Transnational Activities

Advancements in communication technologies have transformed the adaptation of immigrants in the host country and the nature of their ties with the home country. Lower travel costs allow more movement of immigrants across borders. For these reasons, immigrant adaptation in the new country is now "the process by which transmigrants, through their daily activities, forge and sustain multi-stranded social, economic, and political relations that link together their societies of origin and settlement" (Basch et al. 1994: 6). This definition focuses on the ties and activities of immigrants in multiple locations. In other words, ties with the home country remain strong even after immigrants have been integrating into the host country for a long period. In this context, immigrant communities do not simply help immigrants adapt; they also help facilitate transnational ties between immigrants and their home countries.

Transnational contact and networks help immigrants connect to the home country despite their physical absence. Immigrant communities often play a critical role in facilitating transnational contact and networks. Community organizations regularly invite guests, from NGO leaders to movie stars from the home country, to visit, hold forums, and present shows. Ethnic radio and TV stations provide updates on the most recent developments back home with live interviews. Churches hold special meetings and gatherings for their congregations, led by preachers from the home country. Government representatives from the home country may visit to discuss major initiatives there. All of these activities keep immigrants up to date and closely connected with their home country.

Immigrant communities also facilitate transnational economic activities. Chapter 5 explores how these ties are becoming an increasingly important part of ethnic economy and immigrant businesses. Portes et al. (2002) defined transnational entrepreneurs as those whose businesses require them to travel frequently and conduct business activities across borders, usually in the home country and the host country. For example, Dominican immigrants in New York City operate transnational couriers between the Dominican Republic and the United States, and the number of shops selling Dominican products in New York City is increasing (Yang and Wang 2007). Chen and Tan (2009) found that many Chinese immigrants in Toronto used their social networks back home in their import–export businesses. Saxenian and Edulbehram (1997) found that immigrant entrepreneurs like engineers and scientists in Silicon Valley relied heavily on their professional networks back home to promote their businesses. However, in their study based on data collected from respondents of three groups, from Colombia, the Dominican Republic, and El Salvador, Portes et al. (2002) reminded us that only a small proportion of immigrants are involved in transnational economic activities. They are usually self-employed and living in immigrant communities with institutional supports.

Immigrant entrepreneurs use their networks in immigrant communities to maintain and expand their transnational social and business networks. The transnational networks developed in immigrant communities help them develop clients, expand business opportunities, and explore ways of lowering production costs through networks in multiple locations. For example, they may expand their customer base back home by connecting with new friends through social functions or business associations in the host country. Landolt (2001) focused on Salvadorians in the United States, and found that transnational institutions in immigrant communities usually involve three factors: financing, production, and markets. Financing can be drawn from various locations in flexible ways whenever needed; resources and manpower for production can be obtained from whichever side has lower costs; and markets can expand by reaching customers in multiple locations. These factors allow institutions to maintain their transnational economic activities and sometimes strengthen them over time.

Immigrant communities also help promote transnational political activities, supporting or opposing the ruling government of the home country, and/or targeting specific events or policies. Transnational political activities are generally supported from two sources. First, many are organized through non-governmental organizations (NGOs) based in immigrant communities. These NGOs organize activities to promote awareness, lobby the receiving country to support or oppose certain events, and raise funds to support activities in the home country. They may work only with co-ethnic members, or may work with international NGOs to exert pressure on the government back home.

The government of the home country may also try to connect with emigrants through various activities in immigrant communities: speeches, financial support for community events, or workshops to explain newly adopted or proposed policies. These efforts demonstrate that most governments recognize the extensive transnational ties of most immigrants, and that gaining their support may help win the support of their relatives and friends back home.

Some transnational activities organized in immigrant communities also shape the social wellbeing of children. Exposure to information about their parents' home country can keep them interested in it, and community activities involving contact with the home country can help them maintain their ethnic identity. The transnational ties that they develop through their parents may also provide alternative career paths, so some may choose to work in their parents' home country after graduation.

Conclusions

Our understanding of immigrant communities has changed over time. Most early studies explained the experience of European immigrants in North America by emphasizing the goal of easing their adaptation to the new country. Today's scholars are focusing on both easing their adaptation and maintaining their transnational social and economic ties. In addition, our understanding of immigrant businesses has also shifted: from poor communities with limited resources to communities with socioeconomic diversity and multiple locations. All of these changes also reflect larger changes in terms of the diverse socioeconomic and demographic backgrounds of immigrants.

There is little doubt that the increasing diversity in the membership and function of immigrant communities has had important effects on how immigrants adapt to a new society. On one hand, the diversity can translate into access to a variety of resources, more social support, and protected markets; in turn, the immigrant community can become a strong conduit for immigrants to obtain economic and political gain. However, the diversity and self-contained environment of immigrant communities can easily trap immigrants into social separation, which in turn may affect their social integration into the wider society.

Our discussion has noted that the facilities and resources offered by immigrant communities can affect the social and economic wellbeing not only of immigrants, but also their children. Members of the second generation may have the choice to move to the country of their parents' birth, or to move between the two countries. This situation can be advantageous by providing alternative paths to economic success via transnational ties.

At a time when immigrant communities are found in most major immigrant destination cities, their role becomes more important than ever. However, the diverse economic background of immigrant communities and their various locations seem to suggest that immigrant adaptation can take many different trajectories. Such suggestions echo strongly the segmented assimilation process suggested by Portes and his colleagues (Portes and Rumbaut 2006; Portes and Zhou 1993; Zhou 1997), that there is no single path of integration among immigrants in the current context.

5

Immigrant Businesses and Ethnic Economies

The diverse forms and locations of immigrant communities discussed in chapter 4 has yielded equally varied forms and locations of immigrant business enterprises. Hard work, entrepreneurial spirit, and local and transnational co-ethnic ties have allowed immigrant businesses to become an integral and visible element of all major cities globally. From Frankfurt to Rome in Europe, from Taipei to Singapore in Asia, and from Vancouver to New York in North America, immigrant businesses are a visible presence. The locations and other characteristics of these immigrant businesses have changed over time. When researchers began to study immigrants in cities several decades ago, immigrant businesses were usually small and located within immigrant communities. Today, though some immigrant businesses are still clustered in immigrant communities, many are scattered throughout the city (Fong et al. 2012). Their sizes and the industries in which they are involved are also more diverse (Fong et al. 2008). They may range in size from "mom and pop" convenience stores supported by family members to large high-tech companies with hundreds of employees.

Immigrant businesses are becoming increasingly important. According to a recent 2012 report by the US Fiscal Policy Institute's Immigration Research Initiative, about 4.7 million people, or 14 percent of those employed by small businesses, work in immigrant-owned small businesses (Kallick 2012). The report defines small businesses as having at least 1 and less than 100 workers. Together these immigrant-owned firms generated about

$776 billion in 2007. In Canada, Li and Li (1999) reviewed advertisements in three widely circulated ethnic newspapers to estimate the size of the Chinese ethnic economy in Toronto, and estimated the 1996 revenue from advertisements alone to be at least $34 million. Given that many ethnic businesses do not advertise in ethnic newspapers, the actual economic impact of the Chinese ethnic economy is much larger. Li and Li (1999) only focused on the Chinese community, so the economic impact is even more substantial when businesses owned by other immigrant groups are considered.

This chapter summarizes research on the types and dynamics of immigrant businesses, and how they are related to immigrant communities. It reviews the concepts of immigrant enclave and ethnic economy, which were developed to explain the growing diversity of immigrant businesses in location, size, and industrial sector. It also explores how the city context, such as population size and unemployment level, shapes the economic returns of individuals who participate in immigrant businesses.

Classification of Immigrant Businesses

Most studies have explored immigrant businesses from an ethnic point of view, mainly because most of the ethnic businesses of new immigrant groups are owned or operated by ethnic minorities (Light and Gold 2000). For example, the 2011 Canadian National Household Survey reported that among various ethnic minority populations, including Chinese, Latin American, and Arab, 90 percent of those who were self-employed were recent immigrants. In the US, the 2007 Survey of Business Owners reported that 82.3 percent of Asian business owners were foreign-born (Heimer 2007). The high proportion of immigrants becoming entrepreneurs partly reflects government selection of immigrants with business backgrounds, and partly reflects how immigrants search for alternative paths to economic success as they see that they have reached the ceiling of their career advancement for a variety of reasons, including discrimination (Li 2001; Maxim 1992).

Classification of businesses as "ethnic" has been controversial, because different researchers have used different criteria. Reitz's study of ethnic businesses in Toronto included businesses that used an ethnic language in the workplace (Light and Gold 2000). Bonacich and Modell (1980) defined ethnic businesses as ones that are owned by ethnic employers and operated by co-ethnic employees. Li and Li (1999) defined ethnic businesses as ones that advertise in major ethnic newspapers, stressing the importance of ethnic customers. The most commonly used classification is based on business ownership. If a business is owned by immigrants, it is considered to be an ethnic business, whether or not it employs co-ethnic workers, uses an ethnic language in the workplace, or serves a majority of co-ethnic customers. The emphasis on ethnic ownership of a business suggests that ethnic owners will decide what is best for the business and the extent to which co-ethnic members are involved in business operations, recruitment, and planning (Light and Gold 2000). The ethnic owners will decide what is best for their businesses. This definition of ethnic businesses considers only one co-ethnic business aspect without realizing that the importance of ethnic ownership may be insufficient.

Common Characteristics of Immigrant Businesses

Early research on ethnic businesses emphasized their function as catering to the needs of co-ethnic members who had recently arrived in the new country. Faced with a foreign culture, immigrants prefer a familiar environment. They want restaurants that serve their own cuisine, grocery stores that sell their ethnic cooking ingredients, TV stations that show programs in their own language, and newspapers written in their own language, so they can keep up to date with local and world events. At the same time, newcomers are usually not familiar with the institutions and systems of the new country; they need services to help them obtain information and resources, from healthcare to banking. This focus is on the demand side of the explanation (Light and Gold 2000). Thus, most early studies explored immigrant businesses located within immigrant communities.

Immigrant businesses are usually small in scale, as most immigrants have limited financial resources and are constrained in their financial capital; without an established credit history in the new country, they usually have difficulty obtaining loans from established financial institutions (Portes and Bach 1985). Their investment style also tends to suggest that immigrants are cautious about investing in a new environment about which they have limited knowledge. To minimize labor costs, business owners usually work long hours and recruit family members, typically their wives and children (Park 1997). If they decide to employ additional staff, they try to reduce recruitment costs by finding new workers through friends and family members. To reduce recruitment costs, they seldom go through formal recruitment channels or agencies. Despite the lower cost of recruitment, recruitment efforts based on social networks can enhance the performance predictability of employees, because their backgrounds and abilities are usually known in the network (Zhou 1992). Additionally, though ethnic-based networks usually recruit co-ethnic employees, co-ethnic employees are actually preferred, as most of the customers are co-ethnic members, and selling the products requires ethnic-specific knowledge (Waldinger 1986).

A common obstacle to the sustained growth of immigrant businesses is that the majority of their customers are usually co-ethnic members. A finite number of potential customers can support only a limited number of businesses, so some immigrant businesses expand their markets by expanding beyond their own ethnic community. This expansion is also supported by increased demand for ethnic goods in the wider society and the increasing aspirations and agency of immigrant entrepreneurs. Increasing availability to outside markets through financing, sophisticated marketing, and distribution strategies such as franchising has helped many immigrant entrepreneurs reach wider markets.

Market expansion by immigrant business owners can take several forms, each with its own risks and rewards. First, immigrant business owners may carefully select locations outside the ethnic community where competitors are not already operating; this can help ensure a sufficient flow of customers who desire the product and have the disposable income to purchase it (Min 1996). Second, rather than finding a new location, immigrant business owners may seek to undercut existing competitors by offering products or services with lower profit margins (Min 2008). If successful, this strategy may put competitors out of business and attract a wider base of customers who were previously unable to purchase the product. However, a "race to the bottom" in a price war can be unprofitable and difficult to sustain in the long term; it can also lead to ill-will among competitors. Third, immigrant businesses can explicitly focus on targeting ethnic products and services at non-ethnic customers, featuring only the ethnic products that non-ethnics find appealing. Some ethnic products can be hybridized with other non-ethnic products to find greater appeal, or retail environments can be designed with non-ethnic customer tastes in mind. This strategy can help expand the customer base to outside the ethnic community where competition may be less fierce, but also retains the advantage of using the immigrant's ethnic-specific knowledge. A fourth approach is to avoid competition with other immigrant businesses by entering an industry that does not usually include immigrant businesses. This approach requires identifying opportunities where existing businesses are averse to change or unwilling to adopt new technologies, or supply-chain improvements that the immigrant business owner would be willing to implement.

The next sections explore how social scientists have adapted and expanded the concepts of immigrant enclave and ethnic economy to explain why immigrant businesses are now being found in increasingly diverse locations and industries. The concept of immigrant enclave helps explain the geographic clustering of immigrant business activities, and the concept of ethnic economy helps explain the concentration of co-ethnic owners and employees in different industrial sectors, and the dynamic interrelationships among these different ethnic businesses, their owners, and their employees.

Immigrant Enclave Economy

The concept of the ethnic enclave was first introduced in the 1980s, when Portes and colleagues studied Cuban immigrant businesses in Little Havana, Florida. Portes defined ethnic enclaves as "immigrant groups which concentrate in a distinct spatial location and organize a variety of enterprises serving their own ethnic market and/or the general population" (Portes 1981: 290–1). A cluster of immigrant businesses can be considered an ethnic enclave if it meets three conditions. First, ethnic businesses are clustered geographically in a particular location. Xie and Gough (2011) argued that spatial clustering enables immigrants to use ethnic resources to support their daily operations, recruit employees, and retain customers. Second, ethnic businesses are involved in diverse industrial sectors, providing services to meet the diverse needs of their immigrant community (Portes and Bach 1985). Services in close proximity to one another encourage the flow of co-ethnic customers, and a larger ethnic enclave implies more social enclosure of immigrants, who do not need to seek services outside their ethnic community. Third, an immigrant enclave serves not only co-ethnic customers, but also customers from the wider society. The services and activities in the immigrant enclave are tailored not just for co-ethnic members, but also for the general population, in order to maximize the potential customer base.

The theoretical construct of the ethnic enclave is based largely on the dual labor market theory, which acknowledges the co-existence of two labor markets in each city (Sanders and Nee 1987). Immigrants usually work in jobs characterized as undesirable and unstable, with little career advancement. Local-born workers are usually employed in another set of jobs, which usually have more opportunity for career advancement and associated job benefits. These two labor markets are largely independent, and workers seldom move from one to the other. From this theoretical perspective, ethnic enclaves are considered to be another labor market in the city that co-exists with the dual labor market.

Portes and Bach (1985) went on to argue that working in ethnic enclaves can lead to positive outcomes for immigrants. Their earnings are compatible with those outside the ethnic enclave. The earning patterns suggest immigrants can draw from ethnic resources to get ahead in the new society instead of being stuck in the wider labor market with undesirable jobs and no future. The implications of this conclusion challenge a common understanding of assimilation, that immigrants have to give up ethnic ties in order to assimilate into the new society (Waldinger and Lichter 2003). Other scholars have since built on Portes' research, focusing on Chinese in New York, San Francisco, and Los Angeles in the US, and Vancouver and Toronto in Canada (Fong and Lee 2007; Li and Li 1999; Sanders and Nee 1987; Zhou and Logan 1989). Some scholars have focused on other groups, including Koreans in New York and Los Angeles in the US, and Toronto and Vancouver in Canada, but their results do not support those of Portes and Bach (1985).

Drawing largely from the perspective of class struggle, Sanders and Nee (1987) found that the economic returns of individuals working in immigrant enclaves was positive for employers, but not for employees. They suggested that co-ethnic employees were subjected to exploitation as they were bound by ethnic patronage and limited employment opportunities outside the immigrant enclave. A later study by Chiswick and Miller (Durington 2006) also found that individuals working in an immigrant enclave earned less. Zhou and Logan (1989) used residence as a proxy for enclave and found that earnings were positively related to human capital for males, but not for females; the authors suggested that many females might be helping their families with minimum wage jobs. However, these studies may suffer from selectivity issues, because individuals working in immigrant enclaves are not random populations. In Sweden, a government program distributes refugees randomly, allowing the enclave effect to be tested independently from selection. Scholars have found that this program increased the income of refugees by about 4–5 percent (Rumbaut 2008; Xie and Gough 2011).

In short, the dual labor market theory provides a theoretical foundation for the development of ethnic enclaves. However, the original hypothesis that participation in an ethnic enclave can bring positive outcomes is not consistently supported. There is considerable debate about whether the earnings of individuals who participate in an ethnic enclave economy are higher or lower than if they had found work elsewhere. Some scholars argue that ethnic enclaves are beneficial to employers but not employees, and for males but not females.

Ethnic Economy

Logan et al. (1994) introduced the concept of the ethnic economy to understand immigrant economic activities in the city. An ethnic economy has three main dimensions. First, an ethnic economy stresses co-ethnic representation, particularly the representation of co-ethnic employers and/or co-ethnic employees. A highly co-ethnic representation in an industry implies co-ethnic domination of the market, as well as recruitment and daily operations through co-ethnic ties. Co-ethnic employees may be shielded from possible discrimination because of co-ethnic domination, but some contradictory evidence suggests that co-ethnic employers may benefit at the expense of co-ethnic employees (Kwong 1996; Portes and Bach 1985).

The second dimension is concentration: concentration within the entire city, not just spatial concentration in one particular region of a city. Here, the focus is at the city level because the labor pool and customer base for ethnic businesses are usually the ethnic community of the wider city, regardless of geographic location.

The third dimension is sectoral specialization, which implies the presence of an ethnic network within certain industries, which in turn gives co-ethnic members an advantage in coordination and accessing information and resources. This over-representation of co-ethnic employers and/or employees within an industrial sector encourages a "cultural division of labor" (Chao 1996) along racial and ethnic lines and minimizes direct competition among groups. Recent immigrants have less ability to compete in the labor market; a protected niche of industry can shield them from competition and minimize their disadvantage.

Fong and Shen (2011) observed similar results in large Canadian cities. They found that the number of ethnic employees working in an industry was proportional to co-ethnic business ownership in the industries, indicating that these businesses provide job opportunities for co-ethnic immigrants. However, over-representation in specific industries reflects the educational backgrounds and skill levels of immigrants. Wilson (1999) differentiated industry-specific occupational niches can act as important ethnic-protected working environments. Ethnic occupational concentration enables enclosure of the working environment for ethnic members at the organizational level. It also is related to the strategy of developing "a territorial organization" (Park 1936b).

Light and Gold (2000) suggested a theoretical foundation for the ethnic economy based on the "middleman minorities" model, which describes how marginalized minorities organize and concentrate their trading in certain industries. This model has been used to describe the economic activities of certain groups throughout history, and Light and Gold argued that it is also applicable to the current concentration of co-ethnic employers and employees in certain industries. Such industrial concentration is similar to the historical operation and dynamics of these middleman businesses. For Light and Gold (2000), the ethnic economy is largely a case of middleman trading.

Using their definition of ethnic economy, Logan et al. (1994) found that immigrant groups were over-represented in a range of industries within a number of American cities, and that these industries differed between cities as a result of demographic and social differences. Fong and Shen (2011) explored the ethnic economy of new immigrant groups in Canada and published similar results. Both studies found that only a few industrial sectors had a high concentration of both co-ethnic employers and employees; both studies found that it is unusual for both co-ethnic employers and employees to be concentrated in an industry.

In recent years, immigrant economic activities have been increasingly described in terms of ethnic economy rather than immigrant enclave. Akin to the expansion of immigrant activities outside the traditional territory of the enclave, ethnic economy better describes the engagement of immigrant businesses with co-ethnic and non-ethnic urban and suburban communities throughout a city. Studies of the ethnic economy are also facilitated by the availability of data, such as Census counts on the distribution of each ethnic group by industrial sector and class of worker. These data can allow estimates of the extent of over- or under-representation of each group by industrial sector at the city level. However, it is more difficult to find rich data about immigrant businesses in specific geographic areas within a city, which are essential for studying enclaves. Researchers are increasingly treating the immigrant enclave as a special topic within the field of the ethnic economy because of these data limitations, and also because the concept of the immigrant enclave can only describe a limited range of immigrant economic activities in contemporary cities. In summary, two concepts have been introduced to capture different aspects of immigrant businesses as a group: one emphasizes the diversity of immigrant businesses involved within a geographic area, while the other emphasizes the immigrant businesses involved in diverse industrial sectors.

City Context and Immigrant Economic Activity: Classical and Contemporary Perspectives

This section examines how city contexts shape immigrant businesses and the economic wellbeing of individuals working in them, presenting three important issues related to the causes, consequences, and dynamics of immigrant business with respect to geographic or industrial sector concentration. The first is the emergence of an immigrant enclave. In particular, we describe how in this early stage, immigrant businesses begin to concentrate in certain locations and industrial sectors in which they are involved. The discussion provides a glimpse of the genesis of an ethnic community in a city. The second is the spatial distribution of immigrant businesses within a city. Research shows that where immigrants locate their businesses is based on distinctive group survival strategies for finding a niche in the city. The third issue is the economic returns for individuals participating in the ethnic economy. For example, are income levels for those with similar education and work experiences comparable among those who are employed inside and outside an ethnic economy?

The Emergence of an Immigrant Enclave

Although many studies have focused on the mechanisms and dynamics of established immigrant enclaves, few have explored the emergence of immigrant enclaves. Most of these have drawn from Burgess's early research on neighborhood change. Burgess (1925) suggested that a process of "invasion–succession" begins with a few minority groups moving into a neighborhood, which triggers the majority group to move out. Burgess focused on changes in residential areas, but later studies applied the same model to immigrant businesses. Aldrich and Reiss (1976) focused on ethnic businesses in Boston, Chicago, and Washington, DC in the 1960s and found that Whites began to move out when minority businesses moved in. Another study of three cities in the United Kingdom revealed similar patterns in ethnic turnover (Aldrich et al. 1985).

However, Burgess's succession model appears to be less useful in describing the emergence of ethnic enclaves in contemporary multi-ethnic cities. A study of Koreans in Toronto revealed that they usually purchased businesses in an area from other non-majority immigrant groups, such as Greeks and Chinese (Fong et al. 2012). In other words, new concentrations of minority businesses often occurred in areas where other minorities were already concentrated, rather than moving into a majority-dominated area. Regardless of whether the succession process occurs in minority or majority-dominated neighborhoods, research has consistently demonstrated that it is rapid once a new group "invades."

The Toronto study also identified the important role played by co-ethnic property owners and real estate agents in the early stages of an immigrant enclave (Fong et al. 2012). The initial growth of

Korean businesses was facilitated by two processes. First, Koreans took over properties from other immigrant groups in the area, transactions that were facilitated by real estate agents who networked within and across both existing and new groups. Second, once the group secured property ownership, property owners sought to subdivide their buildings into smaller units for rental. Smaller units lowered rental rates to levels that were affordable to emerging Korean business owners. Korean property owners were aware of the optimal amount that most Koreans could put forward to start a businesses, and the end result was a dense ecosystem of individually owned ethnic businesses. The clustering that emerged encouraged more co-ethnic customer flow, and in turn more Korean businesses were attracted to the area. This reinforcing process forged a new ethnic identity in the neighborhood, and the dense mix of Korean businesses contributed to its important role in the community and unique look and feel.

In addition to the ways in which immigrant businesses cluster, it is important to identify the industrial sectors involved in the early stage of business clustering. Portes and Bach (1985) found that "retail" and "repair" were the most common businesses in the beginning stage of clustering in the Cuban enclave economy in Miami. These businesses can be considered ethnic-protected sectors, because they mainly serve co-ethnic members, shielding them from direct competition in the mainstream market. They are established to meet the demands of co-ethnic immigrants as they settle in the new country. Zhou's (1992) study of Chinatown in New York City revealed that two industrial sectors commonly found in the immigrant enclave were the ethnic-protected sector and the export sector. Similar to Portes and Bach's findings in Miami, the ethnic-protected sector consisted mainly of businesses that provided daily goods and services for co-ethnic members. The export sector (such as the garment industry) "contains a non-ethnic market characteristic of leftover niches of the larger secondary economy ... that require low economics of scale" (Zhou 1992: 112). Yoon (1997) made a similar observation in his study of Koreatown in Chicago, referring to the obvious presence of immigrant businesses in the ethnic-protected sector.

In short, as the number of immigrant businesses in the area increases, the industrial sectors involved become more diversified. The diversity suggests a growing number of co-ethnic customers. The larger size makes possible the diversity of industrial sectors involved in immigrant businesses, because more customers naturally lead to the development of a critical mass to support diverse types of businesses. The diversity also reflects that businesses are established to meet the growing diverse demands from co-ethnic members as they stay longer in the new country.

Spatial Distribution of Ethnic Businesses

Many scholars have focused on immigrant businesses in ethnic neighborhoods, particularly immigrant enclaves (Yoon 1997; Zhou 1992). Most research on immigrant business locations has investigated the effects of the size of the ethnic population. The relationship suggests that the presence of immigrant businesses requires the support of a sufficient ethnic population. Thus, most studies have focused on immigrant businesses located in areas with high concentrations of ethnic populations. However, most large cities have become more diversified and immigrants have become involved in more services and information sectors, so focusing only on immigrant businesses within ethnic neighborhoods misses where dramatic change has occurred.

Recently, some researchers have begun to examine immigrant businesses located outside ethnic neighborhoods (Fong et al. 2008; Kariv et al. 2010; Li 1998b). Some have also considered the diverse industrial sectors in which immigrant businesses are involved. Fong and colleagues classified four types of neighborhood: ethnic enclave, ethnic clustered, minority, and majority group (Fong et al. 2008). Ethnic enclave neighborhoods have a highly concentrated ethnic population, such as Chinatowns or Italian neighborhoods. These neighborhoods have been studied extensively. The highly concentrated ethnic population means a potentially high volume of customer flow, so it attracts many retail stores and services, including financial, insurance, and real estate services, as well as businesses related to social activities and entertainment, such as movie theatres. The diverse products and services provided in these neighborhoods also attract co-ethnic members who live farther away but visit the ethnic enclave for ethnic entertainment.

Ethnic clustered neighborhoods usually have a highly concentrated ethnic population, but not as high as ethnic enclave neighborhoods. Logan et al. (2002) found that these neighborhoods are usually located adjacent to ethnic enclave neighborhoods, as peripheral areas of the ethnic community. Ethnic grocery stores or restaurants are usually found in these peripheral areas. Most of these are small in scale and require more parking spaces, as it is difficult for their owners to afford the high rents in the central area of the ethnic community. However, their survival depends on strong ethnic networks for recruiting co-ethnic workers and customers, so they cannot be located far from ethnic enclave neighborhoods (Vallejo 2009). As a result, most owners choose ethnic clustered neighborhoods, where they can maximize the co-ethnic customer flow but minimize rental or purchase costs of locating at the center of the immigrant community.

Minority neighborhoods have a larger proportion of minorities. Some immigrant businesses open there to take advantage of the established retail niche and the labor pool of the minority groups. Mainstream business owners may consider the environment of these neighborhoods unfamiliar and therefore too risky, but some immigrant business owners are willing to take the risk. They tend to maintain their profits by offering lower prices to attract minority customers. They usually carry inexpensive products and work long hours with no employees.

Non-minority neighborhoods have few immigrant businesses, and those are usually tailored to mainstream customers rather than their own co-ethnic group. These business owners avoid areas of high ethnic concentration because the jobs they offer are usually less attractive, so they find it difficult to compete with other immigrant businesses for co-ethnic workers. Immigrant businesses in manufacturing sectors are one example; they usually involve long hours and unpleasant working environments. Location in a non-minority neighborhood can maximize the pool of workers beyond their own ethnic group.

The locational distribution of immigrant businesses is influenced not only by the industrial sectors in which they are involved, but also by the size of the business. Small businesses are still the backbone of the immigrant business community, but immigrant businesses are increasingly hiring more employees. This is related partly to economic globalization and partly to changes in the human capital and financial background of immigrants. Small businesses with a few or no employees are more likely to locate in areas with high proportions of co-ethnic members, because immigrants with small operational costs are more likely to take advantage of ethnic resources. Ethnic networks can be critical to these small immigrant businesses for obtaining financial resources, employee recruitment, and training. These resources are created and maintained within their ethnic communities, so the owners of small immigrant businesses tend to need to stay close to other co-ethnic members, associations, community activities, and frequent social interactions. The spatial requirements suggest that these small businesses are more likely to cluster in ethnic neighborhoods. However, because of high rental costs, not all immigrant businesses are located in ethnic neighborhoods. As mentioned earlier, some of them are located near ethnic neighborhoods to maximize proximity and minimize cost.

Some large immigrant businesses are located in areas with higher proportions of ethnic groups, while others are located outside the ethnic community. They can take advantage of their size to exploit the economies of scale and dominate the co-ethnic market through vertical integration, from wholesale to retail, and through horizontal integration, by linking various related services and selling related products. Yet, given their size, these firms require larger markets that go beyond a specific group of customers. Operating businesses outside the ethnic community not only increases the diversity of customers, which suggests potentially larger sales, but also implies a larger pool of potential workers beyond their own ethnic group.

Economic Returns When Participating in Ethnic Businesses

What are the economic returns when participating in the ethnic economy, both as an employer and employee? There are discussions about how factors from individual socioeconomic characteristics and individual social capital to city context affect economic returns. Since this book is about immigration and the city, we focus on the relationship to city characteristics. Therefore, even when discussing individual socioeconomic factors, the focus is on the ways that the city characteristics can shape the relationship between individual socioeconomic factors and the economic returns of participating in immigrant businesses.

Individual Socioeconomic Background and Metropolitan Size

More immigrants are now settling in small and medium-sized cities, and they tend to earn more than immigrants in large cities (Fong et al. 2015; Kitching et al. 2009). The earnings of immigrants in large cities are positively associated with individual socioeconomic status, but this association is weaker in small to medium-sized cities. Better language ability and staying longer in the country are also more strongly associated with higher income among immigrants in large cities than among those in small to medium-sized cities.

To explain these patterns, researchers recognize that large cities typically have a larger presence of immigrants, because large cities usually are their first destination when they arrive in the new country (Fong et al. 2015; Rogoff 2003). Therefore, large cities are referred to as immigrant gateway cities. The presence of substantial numbers of immigrants in immigrant gateway cities suggests the presence of immigrant communities. A vibrant immigrant community helps to maintain a stronger co-ethnic attachment, which can have negative influence on the earnings of immigrant entrepreneurs. It also implies a higher level of ethnic enclosure, which also can have negative influence on the earnings of immigrant entrepreneurs. Yet, co-ethnic employees may not benefit from the situation because only a small number of extra employees will be hired as most employers with limited capital are careful about their business expansion. When a business operates in a socially enclosed environment, business information can be reduced and opportunities can be limited. In addition, a larger number of immigrants implies a higher number of immigrant business owners. This situation creates a more competitive business environment, and so profits can be affected in immigrant gateway cities.

There usually are fewer immigrants residing in small or medium-sized cities. The small number of immigrants working in immigrant businesses in small or medium-sized cities suggests that they are less likely to be bound by the ethnic obligations that are fostered by clear ethnic boundaries. Immigrant employees benefit considerably from the situation. They are less likely to be exposed to ethnic patron relationships that can subject them to exploitation in an ethnic enclosure setting. A smaller immigrant population in small or medium-sized cities also implies less business competition, so immigrant business owners may be more willing to invest in training and retention. They are also willing to pay higher wages to attract immigrants to work there. Immigrants in a small immigrant community in a small or medium-sized city will have more opportunities to interact with individuals outside their own group. The increase in inter-group interaction suggests greater information flow, which can lead to more job information and opportunities. Employers have to pay a competitive market rate to hold on to their co-ethnic employees.

In summary, economic returns for both immigrant business owners and employees are related to the size of the city: smaller cities have smaller ethnic communities, and the smaller co-ethnic labor pool and greater inter-group social integration puts pressure on employers to provide attractive wages and training. Conversely, the lower levels of competition offer potential for wider profit margins. These findings illustrate the importance of city size in shaping ethnic community dynamics and socioeconomic returns for employers and employees.

City Context

The socioeconomic characteristics of individuals participating in ethnic businesses are also related to the city's demographic and social context, and their economic returns are directly shaped by the city context. The reason is that immigrant businesses are embedded in the city context. As Nee et al. (1994: 850–1) suggested, "contemporary ethnic economies are deeply embedded in the metropolitan economy in which they are located." Four aspects of city context are particularly relevant to the economic returns of ethnic businesses (Fong and Lee 2007).

First, the size of the ethnic group is related to the economic returns of immigrants participating in the ethnic economy (Chao 1994). The size of a minority group can influence the level of discrimination against them, which in turn can affect group dynamics in the labor market (Bonacich and Modell 1980). Blalock (1957) observed this relationship in his classic study of Black and White relationships in the US, and Olzak (1992) later expanded on it in her ethnic competition theory to explain ethnic conflict. Native-born workers tend to discriminate against immigrant workers because they fear their economic and social wellbeing will be negatively affected by increased competition from immigrants (Bailey and Gatrell 1995). Substantial empirical evidence supports this hypothesis, although most studies have focused on White–Black relationships. Some recent studies moved beyond the White–Black dynamic and still found evidence to support the hypothesis (Messner and Anselin 2004). As discrimination and competition increase, immigrants may move into the ethnic economy to find refuge from the "protected market," but the ethnic economy may not be able to absorb the increase in labor supply. An abundant supply of labor for ethnic businesses can affect the returns for employees; co-ethnic employers may take advantage of the situation and reduce wages as much as possible.

Second, the level of residential segregation also affects the economic returns of individuals participating in ethnic business (Statistics Canada 1996). As mentioned in chapter 2, residential patterns shape the economic opportunities of minority groups. Studies in the early 1970s showed that the spatial mismatch between residential location and job location seriously hampered the likelihood of employment for Blacks. In the 1980s, Wilson (1987) demonstrated how the migration of Blacks out of Black neighborhoods contributed to the disorganization of the Black community, which in turn affected the attachment of residents to the labor market. In the 1990s and recent years, studies have continued to show how neighborhood contexts can affect the labor market performance of their residents (Statistics Canada 2008; Wilson 1987). However, most of these studies have focused on Blacks in the United States.

Research about immigrant groups has yielded mixed results: some studies have found that residential concentration facilitates economic activity, e.g., Chinese in New York and San Francisco, and Cubans in Miami (Portes and Bach 1985; Sanders and Nee 1987; Zhou and Logan 1989). Others have observed a negative relationship between level of residential concentration and economic activity (Min 1996; Sanders and Nee 1987). Fong and Lee (2007) suggested that these mixed findings may indicate that the economic returns of ethnic businesses are not only linked with residential concentration, but also with interaction between residential concentration and group size (Wilson 2003). Concentration of a minority group can shape the economic returns of those participating in ethnic business only when the group has reached a certain size. A larger size suggests the group has reached a critical mass; it can support and foster more diverse business opportunities such as food, healthcare, and entertainment. A high concentration suggests less competition from outside and clearer business boundaries. Ethnic entrepreneurs benefit from a highly ethnic-concentrated population for a larger volume of sales and profits, while co-ethnic employees take advantage of the high demand for labor, which can lead to higher earnings. However, a smaller ethnic population can support only a limited number of business opportunities, as most ethnic businesses depend on co-ethnic customers. In such a situation, employers will not achieve high earnings, and co-ethnic workers will experience low demand for their labor, which can lead to low wages.

The third city characteristic is relative employment rates. Relatively high unemployment rates among minority groups in cities are common, for reasons such as differences in human capital, length of time in the country, and hiring preferences. Ethnic business employers usually prefer to hire co-ethnic employees, so co-ethnic members are offered more job opportunities in ethnic businesses. This pattern, along with the lower likelihood of employment in the mainstream economy, encourages ethnic jobseekers to seek employment in ethnic business. Because limited jobs are available in ethnic businesses, the economic returns of co-ethnic employees will be affected.

The fourth and final city characteristic is high unemployment rates in the whole of the city. The employment opportunities of groups are strongly affected by the state of the city's economy, through a "queuing" process. Ethnic groups are ranked in the job "queue" by various dimensions, including ethnic stereotyping or statistical discrimination. Immigrants or minority groups usually occupy a position at the end of the queue (Statistics Canada 2008). When a city has a vibrant economy, queuing has less effect on employment opportunities for groups at the end of the queue, because most jobseekers can be accommodated. In contrast, a weak economy with a limited job supply seriously affects employment opportunities for groups at the end of the queue, usually immigrants and minority groups. Their disadvantaged position pushes them to seek self-employment or work in the ethnic economy. This increases the labor supply, which decreases economic returns for employers and employees in the ethnic economy, as more individuals become self-employed or look for work in the ethnic economy.

Conclusions

For immigrants, owning a business or working in a co-ethnic business has long been an important path to economic survival. As the socioeconomic backgrounds of immigrants have diversified, the industrial sectors of immigrant businesses have also diversified.

Scholars have suggested a few different models to clarify the increasingly complex patterns of immigrant businesses. Each of these concepts focuses on different aspects of ethnic business, yet all of them take ethnic businesses as a group to understand their economic behavior as a whole. Following the same line of inquiry, this chapter explored the locational distribution of immigrant businesses of different size involved in diverse industrial sectors in major cities with increasing racial and ethnic diversity. To accommodate the demands that stem from different racial and ethnic compositions, immigrant businesses of certain sizes or involved in certain industrial sectors are more likely found in neighborhoods with different racial and ethnic compositions in order to successfully match the needs of their businesses with the unique sets of needs in the neighborhoods. Finally the chapter discussed the economic returns of individuals participating in ethnic businesses. Overall patterns show that city context can directly or indirectly, through their socioeconomic background, influence the economic returns of individuals involved in immigrant businesses.

The discussion clearly demonstrates that the economic wellbeing of individuals involved in immigrant businesses is closely linked with the city in which they reside. The implication is a sort of ecological understanding of human behavior. Individuals are embedded in the social and economic context of the city, and therefore their social and economic behavior is closely linked to the context. It is a reflection of the larger debate in urban studies that began in the 1980s about the importance of city and neighborhood contexts to understand social and economic outcomes. Immigrants are no different from other residents; their economic wellbeing is shaped by the city context in which they work.

6

Immigrants and the Foodscapes, Playscapes, and Landscapes of Global Cities

Throughout history, immigrants have changed cities in the process of adapting to them. This observation is no less true today than in the past, whether it is in the domain of cultural influences, residential built-form, community organization (chapter 4), or business enterprise (chapter 5).[1] Today's global cities embrace a complex array of immigrant social and cultural influences, and openness to the practices, customs, and identities of immigrants is an important factor in attracting further immigration. This kind of openness has risen to new levels due to omnivorous tastes for ethnic and transnational influences by the "creative" elites of global cities,[2] many of whom are immigrants themselves.[3] This chapter discusses the two-way flow of influence between urban society and immigrants, focusing on the domains of food, leisure, public space, and the built environment. These domains together represent symbolic and social boundaries between groups, but also serve to build bridges of shared cultural ties and meanings. Within each of these domains, the struggles and successes of immigrants reflect themes of adaptation, dual identity, social integration, blocked paths, and acculturation. As a consequence of these struggles, immigrants have played important roles in reshaping what is now considered "mainstream." There are many examples of immigrant influences in foods, festivals, customs, sports, and aesthetic preferences that were first brought into enclaves within cities, but gradually spread into mainstream society.

The first section of this chapter explores the two-way flow of influence between immigrants and food. Immigrant-receiving cities benefit from more diverse food and cuisine than other cities, reflecting the mosaic of cultures and the demand for these options (Mazzolari 2012). Food plays an important role in nurturing ethnic community, but is also a vital source of employment and cultural communication with mainstream society. International migration has also played an important role in situating ethnic cuisines relative to national cuisines, as illustrated, for example, by the Chinese restaurant sector in Rome (Mudu 2007).

The second section explores leisure activities in global cities, with particular attention to sports. For example, immigrant and native-born residents in many large cities are getting together in their love for shared leisure activities such as soccer. This process of convergence is traceable to globalization, urbanization, and inter-ethnic contact in cities (Martinovic 2009). The extent of this mixing between immigrant and native-born residents is partially dependent on the social boundaries that are constructed and maintained in public spaces. For example, Trouille (2013) observed a group of Latino immigrant men claiming a contested public soccer field located in an upscale and predominantly White neighborhood in Los Angeles, and explored the dynamics within the group of players as well as discourse with the neighborhood's other residents.[4]

The third section focuses on how the identity and culture of immigrants have shaped the landscape and built environment. Building on the discussion of residential patterns in chapter 2, it will explore how the resources, preferences, and constraints faced by immigrants with different cultural backgrounds influence where they live, their clustering, and how they engage in place-making within the built environment (Agrawal 2006; Harney 2006; Huang 2010; Li 1998a).

Immigrants and the Urban Foodscape

Immigrant food and cuisine has shaped host city foodscapes and residents' tastes for centuries. The ethnic cuisines of immigrants tend to first satisfy demand for ethnic food in enclaves, but many are eventually embraced by mainstream society. Examples of this process can be seen in the mainstream adoption of Italian, Japanese, Chinese, and Indian cuisines. The diffusion of immigrant foods, cuisines, and restaurants into mainstream society is one important indicator of the more general two-way process of adaptation and influence between newcomers and existing cultures (Gabaccia 2000). However, this diffusion is not simply the by-product of natural processes: it requires that social, political, and cultural boundaries are altered and crossed. This "boundary work" is inherent to the challenges and successes of social integration and acculturation. The challenges of adaptation and maintaining dual identity for immigrants are clearly illustrated in the domain of food and cuisine: changing food trends also reflect exogenous global forces changing society, such as transnationalism and the redefining of cosmopolitanism around foreign and omnivorous culinary tastes.

Immigration has important influences on culinary diversity and related employment in the city. First, global cities, and urbanized societies in general, have experienced a proliferation of diverse ethnic foods. Mazzolari and Neumark (2012) found that immigration rates are positively associated with the variety of ethnic restaurants. Second, in addition to satisfying the demand for ethnic foods from co-ethnic and other populations, ethnic restaurants are an important source of employment to new immigrants and offer business opportunities to immigrant entrepreneurs, as discussed in chapter 5. The restaurant labor force is immigrant-intensive in part because immigrants tend to have fewer opportunities in other mainstream job sectors, but immigrants also have a comparative advantage in the production of ethnic food from their country of origin, encouraging immigrant entrepreneurialism focused on the supply of ethnic food. Production, supply, and distribution businesses begun by immigrant entrepreneurs in the food arena provide a valuable model for successful larger enterprises in other fields.

The availability of a variety of food is a positive selling point of contemporary city life: residents of multi-ethnic cities cite the diversity of ethnic cuisines as a positive aspect of quality of life (Cowen 2012). In this sense, diversity offered through immigrant cuisines is a benefit in and of itself. The increased food and cuisine diversity in immigration-intensive global cities is an increasingly important part of the cosmopolitan vision of urban sophistication. Cities that seek to establish attractive communities to high-margin "creative economy" employers have discovered that the employees that work in these businesses tend to favor a diversity of food and cultural options in their neighborhood. Richard Florida (2009) reported that unlike the elites of past generations, the elite "creative" class of today embraces a cosmopolitan ideal that emphasizes the offering of authentic multi-ethnic foods to satisfy omnivorous tastes.

Economists have also investigated the potential benefits of food diversity in global cities. In addition to linking cosmopolitan tastes with omnivorous offerings, economic models suggest that the products and services that flow from ethnic diversity often increase overall national welfare in other ways. Building on the work of Krugman (1979), Broda and Weinstein (2006) reported a net positive effect of differentiated goods from immigrants on national welfare in the United States. Lazear (2000) suggested that the gains from diversity are greatest when groups have information to share that is: (1) distinctive, (2) relevant to one another, and (3) can be learned by the other group at low cost. Ethnic cuisines serve as a good example of diversity benefiting everyone. Cuisines are initially distinctive cultural knowledge, but are embodied in a product relevant to everyone through compatible tastes, and eventually accepted and distributed to mainstream society through accessible forms that can be prepared by anyone (e.g., mass corporate production of foods like spaghetti, bagels, corn chips, and salsa). One by-product of nations with a long-standing history of multi-ethnic immigration is a "culinary" cultural capital that conveys an image of accessibility, receptivity, and diverse food offerings for both upscale and downscale consumers.

Immigrant cuisines must overcome challenges as they make their way into mainstream culture, and successful ethnic food entrepreneurs often need to adapt their cuisines to suit local tastes, moving away from serving other co-ethnics in enclaves and expanding into the city and mainstream society (Gabaccia 2000). Historically, many immigrants first brought their cuisines into inner-city ethnic enclaves where others were most likely to settle, focusing on affordable menu offerings. Names like Little Italy and Chinatown were often applied more by outsiders to exclude, rather than applied by insiders to embrace and protect. Ethnic cuisines have been embraced by non-immigrants slowly and with substantial trial and error, first within ethnic villages, and eventually meeting the critical mass of demand and capital to expand to neighborhoods outside the enclave (Mudu 2007).[5] Today, many of the most prominent traditional enclaves function in name only, still offering a range of ethnic cuisine, but with a clientele that is much more mainstream. The mainstreaming of ethnic cuisines also leads to diversification in menus from upscale to downscale.

Contemporary patterns of ethnic cuisine introduction differ in three key ways. First, much immigration to global cities today is directly to the suburbs. Compared to traditional inner-city receiving enclaves, the suburban foodscape is often dominated by large chain restaurants and stores, creating unique challenges and opportunities for immigrant entrepreneurs. Second, contemporary immigration into global cities is also more diverse from a social class perspective. Some immigrants are refugees who are penniless and limited in their locational choices, while others quickly achieve homeownership status in chosen communities. These varied strata of immigrants bring equally varied demand for upscale to downscale cuisine. Third, terms such as "global," "foreign," and "ethnic" are now associated with cosmopolitanism, and elites from all groups are especially receptive to the introduction of ethnic cuisines, especially when they are hybridized with other cuisines.

Immigration and foreign influences play important roles in global city foodscapes, both down- and up-market offerings. The foodscapes of global cities today are heterogeneous: "foreign," "ethnic," and "international" eateries are key markers of a multicultural urban culture and cosmopolitan lifestyle. Elements of global city foodscapes range from multinational chains like

Starbucks to small local boutique restaurants to the high-end projects of celebrity chefs (see Watson 2006). With regard to visible trend-setting categories of cuisines, urban foodscapes in global cities closely reflect the patterns of elite migration and the prevailing international flow of capital, proprietors, and consumers. They have a transnational as well as a local geography. The ways in which foreign cuisines become embedded in the larger urban foodscape are tied to both the types of producers and types of consumers who act as the driving forces in a culinary field or scene.

Farrer (2010) analyzed the complex culinary politics that produces globalized urban foodscapes. First, he emphasized that consumers use the consumption of foreign cuisine as an indicator of their cosmopolitan identity. As trend-setters through their culinary consumption, they play an important part in adjudicating and authenticating cultures of good and bad taste. In a world of diverse travel and tourism, foreign consumers, international migrants, and elite visitors also play a role in shaping the foodscapes of the global city through their conspicuous culinary consumption. Second, he noted the role of the urban cultural politics of planners and designers in producing the "global city" as a space of cosmopolitan consumption and thus facilitating the place-making of foreign chefs and restaurant entrepreneurs. Examples of these efforts include public expenditure on developing new communities featuring ethnic food markets and restaurants, showcasing multicultural food through festivals, and the protection of multi-ethnic food destinations. Traditional farmers' markets and small merchant districts focusing on food products, such as New York City's Union Square Greenmarket, Singapore's Kreta Ayer Wet Market, or London's Borough Market[6] actively promote the mosaic of food offerings within. Broad desire to foster cosmopolitan food consumption plays a role in public envisioning of new communities and public spaces. There are countless examples of public prioritizing of multi-ethnic offerings in redevelopments, such as Toronto's Harbourfront world showcase market, or the emphasis on gardens of the world at Wychwood Art Barns in Toronto. Even shopping mall food courts are being branded around offering pan-ethnic choices.

Gabaccia (2000) described the rich history of ethnic mingling and borrowing in terms of the culinary traditions of multiculturalism expressed in cities. Successive generations of residents of immigrant-intensive cities have experimented with their new neighbors' cuisines. Compared with other realms of life, food and cuisines have always been a relatively open marketplace for expressing identities and building relationships. Participants in this kind of marketplace include enterprising immigrant cooks and grocers, street vendors, and restaurateurs. Immigrants have cultivated and changed the tastes of city dwellers and nations since the seventeenth century. Immigrant cuisines and foods have also been "Americanized" through the mass corporate production of spaghetti, bagels, corn chips, and salsa, obliterating their ethnic identities. These globalized commodity food products of ethnic origins are traceable to the initial urban immigrants who introduced the original foods to city dwellers. In this sense, entire nations that can purchase these common products are benefitting from the essential urban processes of culinary adoption and diffusion. In today's complex globalized, corporate foodscape, "Americanized" foods like SpaghettiOs® coexist with painstakingly pure ethnic dishes and creative hybrids.

At the lower end of the city foodscape, immigrants have played important roles in street food and vending (Taylor et al. 2000). Street vending was once considered a lower-class business and mainly involved Jewish and Italian populations in the late nineteenth and early twentieth centuries. During this period, street food vendors mainly sold farm products, usually fruits and vegetables, from horse-drawn wagons. Today, street food vending incorporates a diversity of cultures and food selections that reflect the diverse tastes and lifestyles of global cities. From beginning by predominantly offering one food (e.g., ice cream or hot dogs), food carts now offer a variety of foods, including many ethnic foods popular in specific locales. Street vendors may also be subjected to regulations, which they do not always follow. In New York City, the number of applicants for street food vending licenses exceeds availability, so regulations are often ignored: vendors continue to sell food illegally as they remain transient to avoid prosecution.

Food vendors represent a variety of ethnic groups and often view peddling as a temporary job and the first step into the job market. Interestingly, despite their prominent role in developing countries, female street food vendors are largely absent in global cities. The customers of street vendors are typically people who work downtown, as well as students and shoppers in the area. The ethnic diversity of street food options is not necessarily the result of ethnic demand by different immigrant groups, but is often the result of the comparative advantage immigrants have in producing this food, along with the growing demand for diverse products in global cities.

Immigrants and the Playscape

A sizable body of research has examined immigrant leisure participation (Doherty 2007; Stodolska and Alexandris 2004; Tirone 1999). Leisure activities may bring together diverse people to embrace a mainstream lifestyle, but may also facilitate networks within immigrant communities, as some immigrants embrace their ethnic subcultural identity by maintaining leisure separation from the mainstream culture (Stodolska and Alexandris 2004). Leisure-time activities that cut across ethnic and immigrant boundaries are believed to be an important opportunity for achieving social integration (Müller et al. 2008), but the rates of immigrant participation are often low (Frisby 2011; Gobster 1998).

Drawing from work on assimilation and acculturation, a number of explanations have been offered to account for immigrant participation in leisure activities (Elling and Claringbould 2005; Frisby 2011, Gobster 1998). The barriers to participation are complex, reflecting the influences of individual identity, views of outsiders, the sites of activity, environmental barriers to engagement, and the nature of particular activities. Patterns of leisure reflect both decisions and preferences endogenous to the immigrant group as well as exogenous mechanisms of exclusion.

Stodolska (1998) described three dimensions of assimilation that constrain immigrant leisure participation. First, the degree of acculturation (changes in cultural patterns of immigrants to those of the host society) can affect preferences and normative understandings of leisure and thereby influence participation. Second, structural assimilation (the process of large-scale entry into cliques, clubs, institutions of the host society on a primary group level, as well as economic adaptation) is a slow process as contacts and social networks develop outside ethnic groups. Third, behavioral-receptional aspects of assimilation (prejudice and discrimination from the receiving country) deter inter-ethnic leisure and encourage within-group activities. Reflecting these three dimensions, factors known to be correlated with immigrant non-participation or exclusion include language difficulties, unfamiliarity with the specific sport-related activities, prejudice related to their cultural differences from mainstream peers, cultural preferences for certain sports, beliefs about the value of sport participation relative to other activities, involvement in the ethnic economy, and residence in immigrant enclaves (Doherty 2007). Martinovic (2009) found that many of the key markers of assimilation are important for inter-ethnic leisure contact: having a native-born partner, avoiding ethnic enclave residence, speaking the language of the host country, and having completed education in the host country all lead to more inter-ethnic leisure contact over time.

The role of leisure activities in the internal dynamics of immigrant communities can be quite complex, with social class having an important interactive effect on the leisure integration of urban immigrants. Affluent immigrants, many of whom interact with the mainstream population at work, reported the least constraints on leisure (Marshall et al. 2007; Stodolska 1998). For example, among Korean and Polish immigrants, social class has important implications for participation in sports activities (Stodolska and Alexandris 2004). Middle-class immigrants often become more active upon arrival, embrace the new lifestyle, and use sports as a way to acculturate to life of the White middle-class mainstream. Lower-class, blue-collar workers often lack the resources, especially time, and interest to embrace mainstream culture and be physically active. These interactions between immigrant status, socioeconomic status, and intergroup contact both at work and during leisure demonstrate the complex and varied patterns of shared intergroup leisure within any global city.

Depending on the activity and context, leisure activities may also serve to maintain ethnic identity (Hay 1997; Pescador 2004). Stodolska and Alexandris (2004) found that not all physically active immigrants assimilate into the mainstream: many assimilate to their ethnic subcultures in the host society. These subcultures sometimes include sports that are not necessarily popular in the home country but become popular in the immigrant community. Stodolska and Alexandris reported that for Koreans, this was tennis and golf, while for Poles it was fishing. Another reason for differential uptake in particular sports is that the reasons for participation in sports may vary between immigrants and non-immigrants. For example, Yan and McCullagh (2004) found that Chinese-Canadian immigrants tend to emphasize individual health and wellbeing, favoring individual sports over the team sports that many non-immigrants tend to prefer.

Greater immigrant emphasis on educational attainment, family-based leisure, and work in the ethnic economy can also hamper immigrant leisure participation. These emphases reflect different values, but may also reflect unease with interacting with outsiders. Residents of ethnic enclaves may feel more restrained as they view mainstream society as more hostile and threatening, and therefore may not feel at ease among the mainstream population. Fong and Ooka (2006) reported that working in ethnic economies, which usually involves living and working in ethnic enclaves, hampers social integration of immigrants in mainstream leisure time activities, suggesting that the social costs of seeking economic advancement through a common "alternative avenue" of ethnic economy are substantial. Stodolska and Alexandris (2004) also noted that the time-crowding effect of work for low-income immigrants has negative consequences for participation in sports.

Sports can serve as social glue, but can also create and maintain social divides between immigrants and non-immigrants (Friesen and Perreaux 2013). Grey (1992) focused on a smaller city where sports are central to social life, and found that the unwillingness of immigrant youth to participate in school sports has implications in the form of low social status and being perceived as unwilling to assimilate on the terms emphasized by mainstream society.

Racism and discrimination also play a role in patterns of immigrant participation. Tirone (1999) explored the leisure activities of South Asian teens and young adults in Canada, including participation in sports, use of media, and consumer activities such as shopping. Study participants felt that their majority-group peers were racist and/or indifferent to their traditional culture, which made them lack self-confidence about playing sports with the dominant group, even though some were interested in playing. One consequence of this kind of animosity is increased in-group participation, where youth feel they can avoid the racism involved in leisure in the wider community. Tirone (1999) concluded that institutional support is needed to create opportunities for sports participation among immigrants in Canada.

Another body of literature focuses on how neighborhood environmental factors come into play to complicate intergroup participation in sports, such as the role of symbolic power in defining appropriate activities and use of sports fields in contested neighborhood space. The extent of immigrant/native-born mixing in leisure activities is partially the result of social boundaries that are constructed and maintained in contested neighborhood spaces where informal sports take place. For example, Trouille (2013) studied how a group of primarily Latino immigrant men claimed a contested public soccer field located in an upscale and predominantly White neighborhood, shedding light on the interesting dynamics within the group of soccer players as well as between them and the neighborhood residents. Thus, contested space and the role of symbolic power[7] exercised by both minority and majority groups can influence leisure segregation and integration. Eger (2012) focused on pick-up basketball games in different neighborhoods of New York City, and suggested that immigrant background affects the direction of symbolic power: immigrants who are also racial minorities may prefer to play in their own neighborhood's public areas where they have symbolic power, while White immigrants feel more at liberty to frequent different parks.

Despite the significant challenges immigrants face in terms of the social integration of leisure, global cities are crucibles of change. Sports that are largely immigrant imports, such as soccer, which was once marginal in North America, are now mainstream, particularly in large cities. Soccer involves shared cultural affinity, so it is more likely to be a source of contact than other less universally liked sports such as American football. Shared affinity for globalized sports such as basketball also provides an important common activity around which to engage. The increasingly multi-ethnic "majority minority" urban environments have higher rates of intergroup participation than environments dominated by one group, and also have more mainstreaming of global sports such as soccer. This convergence in affinity for leisure activities such as soccer between immigrant and native-born residents in some large cities can be traced to basic influences of globalization, urbanization, and inter-ethnic contact in cities (Martinovic 2009).

Contemporary Urban Landscapes and Immigrant Cultures

Over the past several decades, immigrants have transformed North America's globalizing cities. Urban change has been driven in part by where in cities immigrants have chosen to live and work. The look of many cities has changed with immigrant efforts of place-making to reflect cultural preferences. These distinct forms of place-making can be considered both a response to the realities of social polarization and a reflection of the distinctive cultural practices and preferences of immigrant populations (Agrawal 2006; Harney 2006; Huang 2010; Li 1998a). Place-making is defined as a group's efforts to negotiate an identity and meaning by shaping the built environment and social environment through everyday practices. This negotiation happens between groups in a back-and-forth expression of group identity through a process of debate often called a dialectic. The next section focuses on three kinds of urban landscapes: retail and commercial, suburban, and public space landscapes.

Immigrant Retail and Commercial Landscapes

Given the prevailing patterns of immigrant settlement discussed above, a number of scholars have explored how immigrants have transformed the landscape in efforts to create places that reflect their identities, affinities, and preferred practices (Hall 2011; Preston and Lo 2000). One major focus of research is the suburban shopping centers built by Chinese-Canadian entrepreneurs (Wang 1996; 1999). These shopping destinations have thrived in the "ethnoburbs" discussed in chapter 4, serving as essential centers of community life. These new shopping centers have brought an unfamiliar retail model to Canada, with small units being sold to individual entrepreneurs (similar to residential condos), instead of the conventional commercial North American malls with leasehold arrangements. Asian-themed malls in suburban Toronto are a good example: they represent a different kind of marketplace, similar to retail environments in Hong Kong (Preston and Lo 2000). As with the ideas behind these malls, financing is also increasingly becoming transnational, relying on overseas investment. Globalization has made it possible for extensive networks of capital to extend to these new developments, reinforcing trans-Pacific ties. Immigration, transnationalism, and looser restrictions on capital flow have accelerated the rate of development, and encourage further immigration and investment.

In some cases, new immigrant retail developments have drawn criticism from non-Asian residents for their cultural exclusivity and their effects on traffic congestion in growing communities (Wang 1999). Some have suggested that the rights of developers seeking to serve a particular group appear to trump those who may feel unwelcome or alienated by a new development. These new places reflect the complexities and contestation of meaning, power, and belonging, as local, national, and international influences seek to establish or maintain a dominant narrative.

Suburban Landscapes

Scholars focusing on immigrants and housing in North America's cities have examined the phenomenon of immigrant gentrification of suburban communities. Wealthy immigrants are gentrifying suburban communities, buying a large number of homes and rebuilding much larger "McMansions" in their place (Agrawal 2006; Brosseau et al. 1996). The rebuilding partly reflects the cultural practices and their aesthetic preference. For example, Asian immigrants see their house as a sign of success (Chiang and Leung 2011). A larger home implies economic success. However, many existing residents have criticized this gentrification for changing the character of neighborhoods by replacing smaller homes with larger "boxy" homes that are perceived as inappropriate relative to the size of the lot. Besides these perceived aesthetic problems, the greater likelihood for these larger homes to contain multiple families has stirred debate about fair payment for social services that are drawn from property taxes (Lapointe Consulting and Murdie 1996). Some decry the effect of this gentrification on the affordability of homeownership. Others have debated the extent to which these negative opinions reflect racism toward the largely South Asian-, Chinese-, and Japanese-origin immigrants gentrifying these communities versus the anti-growth sentiment that was present in these communities long before the arrival of wealthy immigrants (Agrawal 2006; Ley 2005; Rose 1999).

Despite these well-publicized examples of wealthy immigrants gentrifying some suburban communities, the reality is that many immigrants rely on rental housing. A number of apartment communities in cities like Toronto are termed "ethnic receiving areas" because they are predominantly occupied by new immigrants. Immigrants to Toronto have dramatically changed the look and feel of communities like Flemingdon Park and St. James Town, which were originally occupied by primarily White families with small household sizes. Today, due to mass immigration and lack of new construction, there is a limited supply of affordable rental housing, and the existing rental supply is often unsuitable. Overall, scholars have argued that minority groups, and immigrants in particular, have fewer rental locations to choose from and are more likely than non-immigrants to experience overcrowded and overpriced accommodation, even in suburban areas (Murdie et al. 1996; Teixeira 2008). It is difficult to assess how much of this crowding and high-priced rents for immigrants is related to structural constraints versus cost–benefit choices to live in pricier and/or more crowded apartments because of the desire for good schools or the acceptance of overcrowding. Because immigrants are more likely to have larger households, they also face greater challenges finding larger apartments because these are scarcer than smaller ones. Some immigrant groups have a cultural preference that all family members stay under one roof despite crowded conditions. Chapter 3 contains a more detailed discussion of extended-family living arrangements. However, discrimination may also play a significant role in where immigrants reside. For example, immigrants are known to face more discrimination from landlords in the rental housing market (Hogan and Berry 2011; Teixeira 2008).

Public Space Landscapes

The built landscapes in multi-ethnic cities serve as a kind of slate on which different groups mark their unique cultural identity. Immigrants work within this "environment of difference" to define their identity. For example, cultural preferences may be exhibited by front and back yard religious decorations by many Hispanic families, or by the Cuban architectural influence on Miami skyscrapers. Boundaries once externally imposed on an ethnic community, such as Chinatown, have been reinterpreted and reconstructed by the ethnic community to celebrate cultural distinctions and generate economic activity. Scholars focusing on ethnographic and social constructionist traditions have explored how immigrants have imbued meaning into urban public spaces, often competing with outside narratives seeking to establish or maintain other identities. Immigrants can assert their presence and identity in a number of ways, by transforming the physical environment (sidewalks, landscapes, storefronts, monuments), by engaging in social environments and social practices within these spaces (ritual and popular celebrations), and via the collective imagination and identification of place. The large multi-ethnic cities in North America today blossom with physical, social, and mental manifestations of immigrant identity.[8]

Meaning-making is a contested process that arises out of discourse between groups, often with different levels of power, seeking to affix their identity to a space for themselves, and sometimes to exclude or ghettoize others. The naming of urban ethnic neighborhoods (Little Italy, Chinatown, etc.) has often been demeaning and pejorative, essentializing differences in cities and drawing boundaries around ethnic groups based on their origin (Harney 2006; Werbner 2001). Anderson's (1991) classic study of Vancouver's Chinatown illustrates how the restaurants, pagodas, and neon lights were largely a Western construction imposed by outsiders, and had little relevance to the Chinese residents and their immigrant experience. Interestingly, although naming immigrant neighborhoods as "Chinatown" or "Little Italy" ignored how residents might define themselves, over time local businesses have learned to manipulate this social construction to attract tourists and maintain more control over the appearance and development of their neighborhood.

To counter outward definitions, immigrant groups use various approaches and practices to make claims to public space in their own identity. Harney (2006) described three ways that Italian immigrants make claims to public space. First, Italians assert themselves through habitual movements that emerge as collective performance, such as an evening ritual walk (*passeggiata*) that serves as a recognizable sign to non-Italians about prevailing ethnic claims to the streetscape. In what Del Giudice (1993) described as the "ethnic personification of space," Italians tend to fix their identity by using architectural features that are reminiscent of Italian styles (e.g., arches, arcades, porticoes, terracotta, tile, marble, stucco), which serve as a symbol of challenging the traditional Anglo-Canadian style. These physical manifestations of Italian identity provide meaning to other Italians, but also cater to the consumption of the urban bourgeoisie. Second, Italian immigrants tend to assert their presence in cities through rituals such as religious processions, sports celebrations, or festivals. Third, Italian immigrants tend to create monuments and institutions within their communities (commercial and/or residential areas) that make claim to space and assert their putative permanence. Thus, Italian cultural and social institutions provide public services and activities in a way that locates the Italian identity ("Italian-ness") on the multicultural map and within public consciousness.

Conclusions

This chapter has reviewed how immigrants influence cities in the process of adapting to them. This two-way process of influence occurs in various ways, but the discussion here focused on the foodscape, playscape, and landscape. Overall, the matrices of influences are complex and varied because the origins, interests, and skills of contemporary immigrants are so diverse.

In the foodscape, traditional models of food being brought into enclaves and slowly becoming mainstream are still relevant, but suburbanization and socioeconomic diversity of immigrant groups have also created newer forms of food and cuisine. For example, the suburbanization of immigrants, many of whom are now more affluent, combined with the elevated status of foreign cuisine by urban elites, has created demand for ethnic food offerings in ethnic enclaves and gentrified neighborhoods, in urban and suburban built environments, and ranging in price from upscale to downscale. Despite these changes, the process of introducing ethnic food into mainstream culture remains the same: it is one part of the more general process of adaptation and influence. Immigrants have long been successful entrepreneurs in the foodscape, as evidenced by the long list of ethnic foods that are now mainstream.

The discussion about the playscape showed how it is often difficult for immigrants to integrate with members of the host society during leisure activities. However, the extent of this integration depends on a number of factors, including time in the country, social class, group size, discrimination, and mutual affinity for popular leisure pursuits. For example, middle-class immigrants often have an easier time acculturating to mainstream leisure choices than blue-collar immigrants, who often lack the time and financial resources, and live in communities with fewer recreational amenities. When there are mutual leisure interests, the resulting social contact can generate connection or conflict depending on the context of that contact. For example, the intergroup discourse among young men vying for control of a soccer field may depend on the relative group position and the contested nature of the activity space. Leisure activities can represent important opportunities for forging social ties and mutual respect. However, they also sometimes maintain ethnic boundaries and solidarity, such as a subculture developing among co-ethnic immigrants based on sport (e.g., cricket).

The discussion of ethnic landscapes showed how immigrants have shaped commercial, retail, suburban, and public space landscapes to reflect their identities, affinities, and preferred practices. For example, suburban shopping centers built by Chinese-Canadian entrepreneurs have thrived in the "ethnoburbs," serving as essential centers of community life. Another important phenomenon is immigrant gentrification of suburban residential communities, buying a large number of homes and rebuilding much larger "McMansions" in their place. Regardless of where immigrants settle, acts of place-making are visible everywhere. They can be seen in the built environment in distinctive forms of retail, signage, housing, monuments, festivals, and other activities. They can also be seen in social rituals within public spaces, such as the collective performance of Italian immigrants' ritual evening walk through their neighborhood. Together, these efforts of place-making represent both responses to feeling marginalized and a natural reflection of distinctive cultural practices and references. The physical, social, and symbolic boundaries created by these actions help locate a specific immigrant identity on the multicultural map and within public consciousness.

7

Time Use among Immigrants: A Window to Acculturation into a New Society

The preceding chapters explored how the process of immigrant adaptation is becoming increasingly complex, as is its relationship to urban patterns. New kinds of data that measure the behaviors of immigrants can help social scientists understand this complexity in ways that were not possible using conventional socio-demographic information from United States and Canadian censuses. This chapter explores how the emerging field of time-use research can help clarify how immigrants adapt. Time-use data can reveal how individuals spend their time and how these behavioral patterns shape their integration patterns, which in turn can lead to the different urban forms discussed in the preceding chapters.

Information about how and where immigrants spend their time in the form of daily routines can complement census data to provide valuable insights. For example, data about what immigrant women do with their time, and how their activities differ from those of native-born women, can reveal much about their assimilation and adaptation to a new society, as can data about how much time immigrant children spend studying compared with native-born children. This chapter will explore how time-use research can help clarify how immigrants structure their daily lives compared with native-born residents, identifying patterns of behavior and settings where activities take place. Time-use data can yield rich information about the daily lives of immigrants in the domains of health, social connectedness, and economic well-being by reporting how much time immigrants spend on these activities. Time-use data can help evaluate whether immigrants are following trajectories consistent with segmented assimilation, classical assimilation, downward mobility, or other models. Unlike conventional structural measures like residential segregation, time-use data can reveal the nuances of micro-level household activities, decisions, and social environments of daily life.

This chapter begins by summarizing the various ways in which time-use data can be used to study immigrant acculturation and assimilation. Next, it discusses the various kinds of time-use data that are available to study immigrant assimilation: qualitative data, surveys with recall questions, and time diaries. It will then explore what time-use research has already revealed about immigrant adults and children, as compared to native-born residents. Specifically, it will focus on time-use research findings about work, sleep, housework, caregiving, family, community activities, and leisure. It concludes by discussing how time-use research can complement other research about immigrant adjustment and adaptation.

Using Time-use Data to Study Assimilation in Terms of Economic and Social Outcomes

Time-use data are useful when evaluating the extent and pace at which immigrants are (or are not) becoming similar to native-born populations in terms of everyday life. Researchers have used time-use data to assess whether immigrants have achieved various outcomes of acculturation and assimilation, and to identify the associated barriers they may face. For example, some scholars have investigated whether immigrants have achieved economic integration by focusing on hours worked (Baker and Benjamin 1997). Others have examined gender differences in economic integration by focusing on how work differs between men and women (Hamermesh and Trejo 2013). Some scholars have studied whether immigrants have achieved social integration by examining leisure activities, community time, housework, caregiving, and volunteering, and how these activities vary over time and by gender (Ribar 2012). Children of immigrants have also been a major focus of time-use research, because this can help reveal their level of commitment to school and their role as links between different cultures. Many scholars have explored the social integration of children by examining time spent studying, at school, at home with family, and outside the home in leisure activities (Kofman and Bianchi 2012).

The increasing availability of detailed time-use data has revealed diversity in time use across immigrant groups. Ideally, researchers should explore this diversity by stratifying analyses in terms of country of origin, generation, and time in the new country. However, parsing the sample by these variables usually leads to subsamples that are too small because immigrants are only a modest proportion of any population survey. As a consequence, many quantitative studies have needed to 'pool' all immigrants into one group for analyses, which has led to generalizations that have turned out to be wrong, with later studies revealing significant diversity across groups (Ribar 2012; Schoeni 1998). When immigrants are divided into different sub-groups, this classification is often based on generation (first, second, etc.). The comparisons that are made depend on the research objectives, but first- and second-generation immigrants are often compared with others who have been in the country for three or more generations. Some scholars have explored how behaviors change with time in the country (e.g., years since arrival).

Immigrant acculturation and integration can be assessed using many different time-use measures, including working hours, family processes, family formation behavior, family structure, marital/non-marital childbearing, parental behavior, intergenerational relations, work/family balance, and health (e.g., obesity). In addition to examining these outcomes, some scholars have tried to identify the most important barriers and constraints to economic and non-economic forms of integration. These barriers and constraints range from micro-level to macro-level factors. Micro-level factors, like household gender role ideology and cultural understandings, influence how men and women interact with the outside world, and what constraints they put on sons and daughters. Meso-level factors, like neighborhood safety or segregation of immigrants from native-born populations, affect whether immigrant children socialize with other children. Macro-level factors, like institutional constraints on foreign degree accreditation, can limit access to certain jobs, in part motivating ethnic economies. Other macro-level influences, like institutional changes in immigration policy, e.g., post-September 11th constraints on labor supply, also affect integration (Orrenius and Zavodny 2009).

Methods of Collecting Immigrant Time-Use Data

Both small-sample qualitative studies and large-sample quantitative population surveys investigating time use help clarify immigrant integration and acculturation. Small-sample studies provide rich descriptive details of time use through semi-structured interviews and ethnographic fieldwork. These studies usually focus on particular immigrant or ethnic groups, seeking in-depth understanding into a few research questions (rather than broad coverage across many topics). These detailed data add richness to the descriptions and context of activities, and often include information about emotional states during activities (using terms such as pleasantness, stress, easy, arduous, etc.). Small qualitative studies can also reveal distinctive time-use patterns among certain ethnic groups that cannot be identified in quantitative studies involving pooled samples of all immigrants. Despite these benefits, time-use data are time-intensive to collect, limiting the sample size and generalizability of results. As with most social science research, the rich descriptions provided by qualitative data need to be complemented with evidence of population-level generalizable patterns and influences based on large samples.

Large-sample studies featuring time-use measures include two types: recall questions from surveys and time diaries. These data are often collected as part of major population surveys by large research organizations, such as the Institute for Social Research or the Census Bureau, and then used by researchers for secondary analyses. Many time-use surveys include both recall and time diary questions. Surveys with recall questions may ask respondents to recall on average how many hours they spent doing a particular activity over a given period of time: for example, how much time was spent each week in paid employment, commuting, household work, outdoor activity, time with children, volunteering, or caring for elderly and disabled relatives. Although recall questions are quick and easy to administer and collect in a survey, they have serious shortcomings. Accurate answers require significant cognitive effort, and responses often involve over- or under-reporting. Responses to some questions, such as time spent with children, may also include a social desirability bias, where normative expectations compel some respondents to over- or under-report the time they spend on some activities (Juster et al. 2003).

Time diaries require respondents to record their activities over a specific period. Respondents describe their activities in their own words, which are later coded by researchers using an extensive list of activity categories. Time diary data tend to be more accurate than data from recall questions, because respondents record when an activity begins and ends. Unlike the limited recall questions, time diaries also allow a respondent to name or describe any activity they engaged in, and to record any other secondary activities they also engaged in, with whom, and where (Zaiceva and Zimmermann 2011). Sometimes, time diary data are combined with technology, like a GPS-enabled activity monitor, to obtain a more complete picture of activity and settings visited over a specific period. Time diaries have several limitations. For example, activities vary greatly by day (e.g., weekend vs. weekday), making it difficult to draw generalizations (Juster et al. 2003). The diaries are also time-consuming to administer, limiting the sample size if substantial funding is not available. Sample-size constraints are an important issue when collecting immigrant time-use data, because immigrant households are only a fraction of the total population and often more difficult to recruit for study. Researchers sometimes seek to "oversample" key groups, such as racial minorities and immigrants, to ensure the sample size is sufficient (Kofman and Bianchi 2012). Despite these efforts, a population survey of several thousand respondents may only include several hundred immigrant households.

Time Use among Immigrant Children

A sizable proportion of children under age 18 live in immigrant families, usually in households within large metropolitan areas. These proportions are estimated at approximately 25 percent in the United States, 33 percent in Australia, and 40 percent in Canada (Katz and Redmond 2010; Passel 2011). The increasing population of urban immigrant children has led to more research about how they are managing, how they differ from other children, and the implications for their wellbeing.

Sustained parental investment is needed to ensure the healthy development of children (Bronfenbrenner 1979). Some scholars have investigated whether immigrant families are providing the developmental contexts needed for their children's learning and wellbeing. Lareau (2011) developed a matrix of interactions and socialization experiences and activities for children; some of these important developmental experiences are tied to learning particular skills or general knowledge, and others are linked with benefits or risks that affect a child's health and wellbeing. Families that structure their children's time to provide them with positive contexts of socialization that build intellectual, social, and emotional competencies, and minimize negative contexts, are making long-term investments in the children's future health and wellbeing. Hofferth and Sandberg's (2001) research illustrates the value of time-use data for capturing the exposure of children to these different developmental contexts.

Time-use research about children generally divides activities into three broad categories: sleep/rest, schooling, and leisure. The most significant differences in time use appear within the "leisure" category, so some researchers have sub-classified this category into: (1) out-of-school learning (reading, homework, etc.); (2) media use (television, music listening, video games); (3) free play (in the street, backyard, at the park); and (4) organized activities (lessons, organized sports) (Baxter 2007). A broad array of household characteristics, family backgrounds, and culturally specific ideals influence how children allocate their time across these different categories and sub-categories. Important household factors include socioeconomic status (SES), maternal employment, and family structure. Higher SES children tend to spend more time doing organized activities, while lower SES children tend to spend more time in free play and media use (Baxter 2007). The high costs of organized/structured activities may explain some of this difference, but higher SES families also tend to emphasize education more. With respect to maternal employment, children of mothers who work full-time tend to watch more television and spend more time at day-care than other children, and also to spend less time reading than children of mothers who work part-time or do not work outside the home (Hofferth and Sandberg 2001). Finally, family structure influences time use. Children in households with a single parent (usually a mother) spend less time learning and more time using media and playing because it is more difficult for a single parent to actively monitor children's learning (Hofferth and Sandberg 2001).

In terms of socioeconomic status, children of immigrants are more likely to be lower SES in aggregate, which is associated with less time spent reading and doing homework outside of school. However, this finding neglects the fact that modern immigrants are socioeconomically diverse in Canada and the United States. Many are middle SES, so many immigrant children benefit from the educational resources of their parents. In 2013, for example, 12 percent of all immigrants were working in management and professional fields. More specifically, Arab-Americans and most Asian-Americans tend to have levels of education and income far above the national average (Ryan and Bauman 2016). Thus, despite their low aggregate-level SES, immigrants vary greatly in terms of the relationship between family SES and children's time investment in education.

Children of immigrants are also overall more likely to have two parents in the household, and to have a mother who either works part-time or does not work outside the home, which is associated with more time spent learning and reading. However, this is not the case for all immigrant groups. For example, Puerto Rican Americans have a much lower percentage of two-parent households than the native-born population.

With the caveats noted above, time-use research suggests that for many immigrant children, the advantages of parental availability may outweigh socioeconomic constraints that some face when it comes to time investment in education. However, the structural constraints faced by some immigrant families can compromise the healthy development of their children by reducing their participation in other positive social activities (Zhou 1997). This is particularly true for immigrants from less-developed countries: many do not involve or supervise their children in organized out-of-school learning activities because of multiple jeopardies of poverty, education, language, and cultural barriers (Borjas 2001; Van Hook et al. 2004). Furthermore, many immigrant parents from less-developed countries engage in service-sector work with non-standard work schedules, which may also hinder parental supervision (Giuntella 2012). However, as mentioned above, children of many immigrant groups are more likely than their native-born counterparts to reside in households with two parents, and this family structure may provide some resilience to socioeconomic disadvantage (Landale and Oropesa 2007).

Another way that immigrant status may affect children's development through their time use is through parenting styles. Immigrant parents may differ from native-born parents in terms of how they think children should use their time out of school. For example, East/Southeast Asian and South Asian children may spend more time reading and doing homework because of the emphasis on educational achievement (Larson and Verma 1999). They may also spend less time in organized sports, which their parents tend to perceive as having little value (Larson and Verma 1999). Children from Latin American or East/Southeast Asian backgrounds may spend more time on family-related activities, rather than free play, because of the cultural emphasis on extended family and close ties among relatives (Foner 1997). The influence of these factors vary by country of origin, as do the norms and cultures of immigrants, helping to reinforce or counteract the structural challenges faced by children of immigrants and affecting their participation in specific activities. Overall, the unique social position of immigrant families within the host society's social stratification system and cultural heritage likely means that immigrant children use their time differently than native-born children.

Time-use studies that have examined immigration status have revealed diverse circumstances for immigrant children, especially with regard to different gender roles, but generally suggest themes of industriousness in school and more time spent on family and culturally specific activities (e.g., language classes). For example, Kofman and Bianchi (2012) found that in the United States, teenage children of immigrants are more likely to spend time studying rather than working after school, and more likely to spend time in family-centered activities, a pattern of activity that exacerbates social segregation from native-born peers but also buffers some of the negative effects of living in disadvantaged urban communities. A study conducted in Australia revealed that immigrant children spend more time in educational activities, organized lessons, and personal care than native-born Australians, a difference that was greatest among non-Anglophone immigrants (Chen 2014). Other studies of children's time use have revealed that the social organization of many immigrant children's activities emphasizes school performance. An American study reported that first- and second-generation immigrant children spent less time than other children playing video games and more time reading and studying (Hofferth and Moon 2012).

The strategy of investing in education is consistent with classical and neoclassical assimilation theories (Kofman and Bianchi 2012). According to this kind of model, educational investment will uniformly help immigrant youths successfully assimilate into mainstream society and experience upward mobility relative to their parents. However, the extent of focus on school is not the same for all immigrant groups. For example, children of Asian immigrant parents tend to spend significantly more time studying than Latinos, who tend to study more than native-born children (Kofman and Bianchi 2012). This evidence of varying investment in education by group is consistent with the segmented assimilation theory (Portes and Zhou 1993). The segmented assimilation theory was developed to address the fact that contemporary immigrants to the United States often assimilate along divergent paths due to segmented opportunities and diverse resources: paths may include conventional upward trajectories, straight-line stagnation, assimilation, downward mobility, and selective acculturation. Despite some evidence of segmented assimilation, the generally high level of school effort among most immigrant children is inconsistent with much downward mobility. However, some immigrant groups may feel excluded from mainstream society, which often translates into less investment in education. Ogbu (1995) found that this kind of academic disengagement is most common among involuntary minorities (e.g., populations who were conquered, colonized, and enslaved, as well as their descendants); they may reject academic achievement because it involves "acting White."

Although it did not primarily rely on time-use data, a recent longitudinal study of immigrant children in New York City provided more optimistic results (Kasinitz et al. 2008). The authors found that today's second-generation immigrants are generally faring better than their parents, with young adults of Chinese and Russian Jewish origin achieving the greatest education and economic advancement, excelling beyond their first-generation parents and even their native-born White peers. More broadly, they found that every second-generation group studied (West Indian, Chinese, Dominican, South American, and Russian Jewish immigrants) is doing at least marginally – and often significantly – better than native-born residents of the same racial group. This held true for the most important domains of life, including economic success: each second-generation group studied earned as much or more than its native-born comparison group, particularly African-Americans and Puerto Ricans, who are generally the most persistently disadvantaged.

Despite the importance of school and studying, immigrant children allocate their time in other ways that affect social integration. One of the most significant differences is in family time and caregiving at home. Immigrant children, especially girls, often devote more time than their native-born counterparts to family and caregiving activities at home. A study of immigrant adolescents in Vancouver, Canada found considerable demand for household work among girls, specifically in the form of caring for younger siblings, ranging from 7 to 37 hours per week (Lee and Pacini-Ketchabaw 2011). Similarly, Mexican immigrant girls living in California spend considerable time doing household chores, caring for younger siblings and grandparents, and even engaging in home-based piecemeal market work to help parents with their market work (Orellana 2001).

Many immigrant children also play vital roles as translators and cultural intermediaries. A study of Yemeni high school girls in Detroit found that most girls spent considerable time caring for younger siblings, translating for older adults, and acting as cultural intermediaries. Immigrant children are valuable help to parents and elders in navigating multicultural city life, reporting time spent reading and interpreting texts, clarifying rules and expectations, and being a conduit for cross-cultural introductions in schools and neighborhoods. Despite their family responsibilities, the Yemeni girls in Dearborn, Michigan, spent more time doing schoolwork than native-born girls, while also taking Arabic classes in the evenings (Sarroub 2001). The tendency for many immigrant children to take language classes and participate in other organized activities focused on their ethnicity and culture is a valuable connection to their family background, but also a source of segregation from mainstream society. A study of Vietnamese youth living in New Orleans, Louisiana, found that 70 percent of girls and 40 percent of boys frequently helped with housework, caregiving, and help with extended family (Zhou and Bankston 1994). Together, these research findings reveal that despite their considerable domestic and family responsibilities, immigrant children tend to complete their homework consistently, which may in part be explained by the fact that immigrant children tend to spend less time than native-born children playing video games and watching television, and more time reading and studying (Hofferth and Moon 2012).

Several studies have used time-use data to compare the health and physical activity of immigrant and non-immigrant children. Many studies have referred to a "healthy immigrant effect" whereby new immigrants maintain healthier diets and rates of physical activity for years after arrival, but eventually develop health behaviors more consistent with native-born populations (Kennedy et al. 2006). Rich time-use data make it possible to situate physical activity along a spectrum, from the most sedentary forms (e.g., television) to most active forms (e.g., sports). Time-use data generally support the healthy immigrant effect. A study of Latin American immigrant children (mostly Mexican-American) in the United States revealed higher rates of physical activity and lower rates of obesity and overweight compared with children born in the United States (Gordon-Larsen et al. 2003). A more recent study with more detailed data revealed that immigrant children tend to spend less time in front of televisions and computer screens than children born in the United States, which counteracts their reduced likelihood of engaging in organized sports compared with children born in the United States (Taverno et al. 2010). Together, these results suggest that immigrant children may have less opportunity for acculturation through organized sports shared with native-born children. The current tendency for many children in advanced urbanized societies to spend a lot of time at home with video games and watching television also works against shared leisure.

Time Use among Adults: Market Work and Barriers to Immigrant Integration

Time-use data related to market work and labor division within households suggest distinctive immigrant approaches to economic integration. Individual and household economic outcomes in terms of income and employment are shaped by decisions about working hours, division of labor, skills investment, borrowing constraints, and commuting times. The standard model of labor supply in economics predicts that the time an individual devotes to work depends on the price of their time (wage rate) and other resources.

Some scholars have applied the "family investment" hypothesis, extending this standard model to test predictions about how immigrant working hours, skills investment, and borrowing constraints compare to those of native-born populations. According to this hypothesis, the spouse with the least long-term wage potential will work more to subsidize the other spouse's skills investment, such as a university education (Chiswick 1978; Long 1980). In other words, families invest in the skills of the partner with the largest wage potential: this could take the form of immigrant adults working many more hours than native-born adults to subsidize the skills investment of a spouse, or the educational success of children. Most research findings support the family investment hypothesis, especially among immigrant households.

Hamermesh and Trejo (2010) suggested that immigrants tend to weigh different assimilating activity options carefully, because they find the cost of engaging in these activities especially high. Fixed costs, such as the costs involved in learning a language or developing more cultural understanding (e.g., working outside an ethnic enclave, shopping in non-ethnic stores) may mean immigrants are less likely to undertake a given activity. However, once they have chosen to invest in an activity, they tend to spend more time doing it. Assimilating activities require energy but tend to pay off quickly. Based on data from the United States and Australia, Hamermesh and Trejo found that immigrants who engaged in this investment process achieved higher wages in a shorter amount of time.

Urban sprawl in Canada and the United States has affected places of employment and residence. It has made commuting an important factor in the integration of immigrants, both as a source of segregation but also a time demand that may affect immigrants differently than native-born populations. Traditionally, immigrants to the United States and Canada resided in enclaves in city centers, close to other co-ethnic populations and job opportunities. This differs from European suburbs, which have traditionally offered more rental housing for lower SES minorities and new immigrants. Recently, the suburbanization of many North American immigrant communities has led to longer commuting times for immigrants. Blazquez and coauthors (2010) suggest that the burden of commuting can influence work decisions in a way that exacerbates residential segregation. A study conducted in New York City revealed that immigrants commuted longer than native-born residents, and were more willing to accept inconvenient commutes. This finding applies to women as well as men: minority immigrant women chose higher wages over a convenient commute, suggesting that they did not have the same liberty as other women to balance domestic and employment responsibilities (Preston et al. 1998). If immigrant men and women are less able or willing to cultivate a work–life balance through shorter commutes, their social integration and acculturation into their community may be challenged because of the work-commute time crunch.

Gender Differences in Work/Home Time

Time-use data can help reveal how and why immigrants divide their time and energy at home and at work. One major theme in this kind of research is the nature of gendered division of labor, and how it affects the social integration of immigrant men and women. For example, more household responsibilities among immigrant women and children may negatively affect their ability to assimilate economically through market work and other activities like school and studying. Scholars have applied time-use data to explore immigrant versus non-immigrant differences in gendered activities (Lee and Pacini-Ketchabaw 2011), household work (Orellana 2001), and establishing enduring social ties in the community (Sarroub 2001; Zhou and Bankston 1994).

Most research findings suggest that immigrant men spend more time engaged in the labor market and less time engaged in housework, community activities, and leisure, compared with native-born men. For women, research findings are complicated by the more nuanced picture offered through qualitative studies. More detailed data and analyses have revealed the need for caution in drawing simple conclusions about immigrant assimilation and acculturation through time-use data. Earlier studies of immigrant women in the labor market pooled all groups together, but more recent studies have revealed important differences among immigrant women. For example, one early study reported that foreign-born White women worked fewer hours than native-born White women (Long 1980). Later, research including more groups and more recent data revealed that immigrant women worked more hours than women born in the United States, but also identified important differences by country of origin: women from the Philippines worked more hours than native-born women, but immigrants from Mexico, the United Kingdom, and Canada worked less (Schoeni 1998). Several reasons may underlie these group differences. First, cultural preference for the homemaker/breadwinner model of household labor division may predominate in certain groups. Second, the economic marginality of some groups may put more pressure on women to work outside the home. Third, some groups may have more access to particular kinds of work (e.g., childcare, construction), making it easier to enter the labor market upon arrival.

Overall, time-use research has revealed larger gender differences within immigrant households compared with native-born households in terms of how spouses allocate their time between market work, housework, caregiving, community activities, and leisure. On average, immigrant women spend more time on housework and caregiving and less time on labor-market work than their husbands (Anastario and Schmalzbauer 2008). Immigrant women tend to spend more time doing community activities and leisure than their husbands, but to engage in these activities less than native-born women (Zaiceva and Zimmermann 2014).

Among immigrants, gender divisions in time use may change depending on how long they have been in the new country. According to classical assimilation theory, gender division should be greatest among first-generation immigrants, with subsequent generation households exhibiting time-use patterns more consistent with those of native-born residents. One study of immigrant married couples from Mexico in the United States yielded mixed evidence (Vargas 2016). The author found that first-generation husbands spent more time on paid employment and less time on leisure, exercise, eating, housework, and caregiving than their native-born counterparts, while their first-generation wives did more housework and caregiving and less paid work than their native-born counterparts. However, contrary to the predictions of classical assimilation theory, gaps between market work and commuting time increased between Mexican-born husbands and their non-Hispanic native-born counterparts over time. In contrast, gender gaps in terms of household work and care narrowed over time. The authors also found that among Mexican-born wives, new immigrants spent the same amount of time in market work and commuting as their non-Hispanic White counterparts, but less time than their non-Hispanic Black counterparts. However, after 20 years in the United States, Mexican-born wives tended to work and commute significantly more than non-Hispanic Whites or Blacks, demonstrating high levels of industriousness, consistent with classical assimilation theory. Vargas (2016) found that Mexican-born wives did more household work than their non-Hispanic native-born counterparts, and that this difference remained constant with time. Finally, Vargas (2016) found that Mexican-born male and female immigrants tend to spend less time on leisure than their native-born counterparts and that this gap increases with time, indicating that their social integration may lag behind their economic integration.

Studies in Europe have also found significant differences in the gendered division of time use in immigrant households. A Dutch study found that Surinamese and Turkish immigrant women differ from Dutch-born women, doing and valuing household work more. It also found that Surinamese and Turkish immigrant men were more oriented to paid labor, valuing household work less than Dutch-born men (Van Klaveren et al. 2011). A study in the United Kingdom found that immigrant women spent more time than native-born women cooking and engaging in religious activities, while immigrant men spent less time cooking and more time engaging in religious activities than their native-born counterparts (Zaiceva and Zimmermann 2011). Later, the same researchers focused on non-market time in the United Kingdom, and found that non-White men and non-White women, many of whom were immigrants, differed from their White counterparts. They reported that non-White men spent more time working and commuting than their White counterparts, and less time using media and doing household work and family care. Non-White women spent less time working and more time doing household work (cooking, caregiving, religious activities) than their White counterparts. One reason for the increased childcare time may have been the higher fertility rates among the non-Whites included in the study (Zaiceva and Zimmerman 2014).

The differential allocation of time spent on market work in immigrant households affects the time parents have to be involved with their children and their school activities, and potential opportunities to engage with other parents and children. The level of income inequality between spouses is an important factor in the sharing of these other responsibilities. A study of Mexican-born immigrants in the United States revealed that parents with more equal incomes also spent more equal time engaging with their school-aged children by participating in school activities and pick-up/drop-off (Hossain and Shipman 2009).

Time Flexibility, Scheduling, and Multi-tasking for Immigrants

Immigrants vary from native-born residents in terms of their time flexibility, work scheduling, and tendency to multi-task. Research conducted in Italy revealed that immigrants are more likely to work non-standard hours, particularly when they are working in the low-skilled hospitality, retail, transport, and manufacturing industries (Giuntella 2012). Non-standard work hours tend to reduce the contact that immigrants have with native-born populations in two ways. First, many other employees working non-standard hours are also immigrants, reducing opportunities for acculturation and bridging ties at work. Second, working non-standard hours often makes it impossible to engage in leisure pursuits with native-born residents, who tend to work standard hours. Thus, this scheduling of immigrant work is a hindrance to social integration.

Another barrier to immigrant social integration is the effect of long commutes on free time. Immigrants, especially those from poorer countries, tend to have longer commutes than native-born residents, often relying on public transit to get between home and work. A study conducted in Madrid, Spain, found that recent immigrants from Africa, Colombia, Ecuador, and Eastern Europe had significantly longer commutes compared with native-born residents and other immigrants. This daily commute reduced the time available for community social engagement outside of work. Commuting time may in part explain the finding that new immigrants tend to volunteer less, although the time they spend volunteering tends to increase with time in the country (Osili and Xie 2009).

A study conducted in the United Kingdom found that immigrant women are less likely than native-born women to multi-task (doing secondary activities at the same time as primary activities). The value of multi-tasking is debatable, but if it does have value, immigrants doing less of it may have implications for getting work done, time management, and balancing competing demands. Although multi-tasking might be an appealing strategy for time-pressed ethnic minorities, immigrants may multi-task less because they have less to gain from doing secondary activities: the opportunity cost for time allocation is higher for native-born women, who tend to have higher socioeconomic status. Also, native-born women may multi-task more because sociocultural norms may have conditioned them to believe that this behavior is acceptable and desirable for accomplishing goals (Zaiceva and Zimmermann 2011).

Conclusions

Scholars need new data on an ongoing basis to assess the complex and ever-changing settlement patterns, community forms, housing adaptations, and household organization of immigrants. Time-use data paints a rich picture of the lived experience of immigrants in contemporary cities, and can help reveal how daily life fosters and impedes acculturation and integration into a new society. This chapter explored several aspects of time-use data and research as they relate to the immigrant experience. First, time use can be studied through both qualitative and quantitative approaches. Qualitative interviews and ethnographic studies allow researchers to investigate what a small group of immigrants do with their time, along with the social and emotional context of these activities. Quantitative approaches, such as recall questions and time diaries, allow researchers to balance a rich recording of daily activities with the opportunity to collect data on a large sample suitable for statistical analyses. Together, qualitative and quantitative time-use data provide rich information about what immigrants do with their time, with whom, and why.

Second, time-use research has helped clarify how immigrant children adjust to a new society, often serving as bridges between their family's culture and a new culture. Most immigrant children seem to have a strong desire to do well in school, as demonstrated by the time they spend studying and engaging in organized educational activities. Immigrant children also tend to spend more time with family and in the household environment; this finding reflects strong family bonds, but also possible challenges with regard to acculturation into the outside society.

Third, time-use research shows how immigrant adults allocate their time to work, home, and community activities, and identifies constraints (such as commuting time) that affect the time immigrants have available for assimilating activities. Immigrant households often divide labor-market and household work in a way that is consistent with the "family investment" hypothesis: seeking to maximize future economic integration by investing in the human capital of household members with the most potential to gain. At the individual level, time-use research reveals that immigrant adults tend to invest their time in fewer assimilating activities because of the high cost, but once they decide to engage in such an activity, they tend to spend more time on it. Although most studies show that women in immigrant households do a greater share of housework and caregiving than women in non-immigrant households, this gender divide decreases with time in the country. Immigrants are also less likely than native-born individuals to undertake multiple tasks at once (multi-tasking), potentially benefitting them with more concentrated effort, but also making it more difficult for them to complete many tasks in a complex society.

8

Conclusions

This book has explored how immigrants experience and organize their lives in contemporary cities. Chapter 2 focused on residential patterns, and chapter 3 focused on housing attainment. Chapter 4 explored the genesis of, and changes to, immigrant communities. Chapter 5 explored economic activities, and chapter 6 discussed how immigration can affect a city's culture, specifically food, leisure, and landscapes. Finally, chapter 7 presented a new type of data that can help clarify the increasingly complex experiences of immigrants: time-use data.

Some of these topics, such as residential patterns, have been explored since the early twentieth century; others, such as cuisine and time use, have been explored only recently. Together, they help reveal how immigrants relate to other groups in contemporary cities, along with the diverse strategies and forms of social organization they may use to achieve desired goals such as economic integration, homeownership, and community.

Chapter 2 showed how residential patterns both reflect and influence the social integration and potential interaction of immigrants with other groups. Scholars have proposed various models to explain the residential patterns of immigrants. In the early twentieth century, Burgess published his classic theory about the role of economic attainment in achieving/increasing social integration. In contrast, Firey emphasized the continuing symbolic significance of neighborhoods and the co-ethnic social functions among neighbors that draw immigrants and their succeeding generations together. The process of ethnic residential mobility and communities in contemporary cities often reflect elements of both of these theories.

More recently, scholars have drawn from the work of Burgess and Firey to develop new theories to explain immigrant residential patterns. Drawing from the work of Burgess, the spatial assimilation theory emphasizes the role of socioeconomic resources and duration in the country in reducing residential segregation among immigrants. Drawing from the work of Firey, the place stratification perspective focuses on why some groups may encounter difficulties moving into neighborhoods that have higher proportions of the majority group. According to this perspective, locations are associated with status and prestige; the majority group does not want to share neighborhoods with disadvantaged groups, and tries to maintain the spatial hierarchy through various institutions. Finally, the group preference theory suggests that residential clustering may be related to individual preferences about living close to one's own group and/or preferences about a particular racial and ethnic composition in a neighborhood.

Empirical evidence provides partial support for each of these perspectives in different contexts. Layers of different processes are likely at work, creating complex racial and ethnic residential patterns. Some studies have explored the effects of diverse racial and ethnic neighborhood composition on group relations. Because most theoretical frameworks focus on majority–minority relations, and the available segregation measures compare only two groups, mixed neighborhoods pose new challenges for researchers exploring the consequences of new residential patterns.

While chapter 2 discussed residential patterns from a macro and historical perspective, chapter 3 examined housing attainment among contemporary immigrants from an individual/household perspective. Housing is not only vital for shelter; it also facilitates privacy, security, belonging, rootedness, neighborly social relations, status, and access to services. An immigrant's housing "career" consists of the series of accommodations attained since migrating, often beginning with modest rental accommodation, but often leading to the widely aspired-to goal of homeownership.

In contrast to the outdated idea of a monolithic immigrant experience, the discussion in chapter 3 revealed that the pathways of housing attainment are now as diverse as immigrants themselves. Immigrant entry classification (e.g., refugee, family, business/economic), socioeconomic status, language fluency, acculturation, and the characteristics of the origin country such as GDP can all hinder or facilitate access to information, housing opportunities, and mortgages. Contextual factors such as housing costs, housing supply, the presence of family and co-ethnic networks, and enclaves within a gateway city also influence housing attainment. National- and international-level factors may also be important: immigration policy can increase or reduce the number of newcomers vying for housing, and outlays for social housing offered to immigrants and refugees can also make a big difference in housing attainment. Case studies have revealed that there are different paths to success: group cultural norms and preferences yield unique adaptive strategies that help group members to navigate the housing market in ways that match their strengths and perspectives.

Despite the housing successes of many immigrants, immigrants are at a considerable disadvantage in the housing market. At the bottom of the housing market, many immigrants face challenges in securing and retaining quality rental housing. Gentrification and the lack of affordable housing development in many gateway cities has resulted in many immigrant families spending a high percentage of their income on rent, or crowding into apartments that are not suitable for their households. Such challenges often lengthen the timeline to homeownership. Both perceived and documented discrimination in the housing market also sometimes limit housing choice, exacerbating the problem of weak attachment to a new society.

Chapter 4 focused on the various forms of immigrant communities. Communities are essential to immigrants, and help shape their social and economic lives and opportunities. Analyses of immigrant communities have changed over time. Early studies focused on the experience of European immigrants in North America, emphasizing the goal of easing their adaptation to the new country. More recent work has revealed the importance of communities in both easing adaptation and maintaining transnational social and economic ties. Also, early studies tended to treat immigrant communities as being poor and having limited resources, but more contemporary work has emphasized their increasing socioeconomic and demographic diversity, robust immigrant business activity, and entrepreneurship in multiple locations across cities. All of these changes reflect larger changes in the diversity of the socioeconomic and demographic backgrounds of immigrants. Immigrant communities can act as conduits for immigrants to obtain economic and political gains, but the self-contained environment of immigrant communities can easily keep immigrants socially separated, which in turn may affect integration into the wider society.

Two recent developments in immigrant communities can increase the chances of economic success: the "ethnoburb" and the increasing role of transnational activities. These can be particularly advantageous to second-generation immigrants by providing alternative paths to economic success in the ethnic community or in the home country. They also add to the vibrancy and growth of the community, making contemporary immigrant communities more appealing destinations for other immigrants. Additionally, the diverse economic backgrounds of immigrants and locations of their communities can lead to numerous possible trajectories for immigrant adaptation.

Chapter 5 examined immigrant business activities and ethnic economies. These are often nurtured by immigrant enclaves, but over time have become more diverse in size, location, global connectivity, and involvement with other ethnic groups. The economic wellbeing of those participating in immigrant businesses is closely linked to the context of the city in which they reside. Immigrants often have limited access to traditional jobs due to language barriers, lack of connections, insufficient educational credentials, and discrimination, so owning a business or working in a co-ethnic business has long been an important path to economic survival. Scholars have suggested a few concepts to help clarify the complex patterns of immigrant businesses. Each of these concepts focuses on different aspects of ethnic business, but all consider ethnic businesses as a group to understand their economic behavior as a whole. Chapter 5 expanded on this line of inquiry to explore the geographic distribution of immigrant businesses of different sizes and in diverse industrial sectors within large cities with increasing racial and ethnic diversity. To accommodate unique demands, immigrant businesses of various sizes and various industrial sectors appear in neighborhoods with various racial and ethnic compositions and needs. Chapter 5 also explored the economic returns of individuals participating in ethnic businesses, which can be influenced directly or indirectly by city context. Overall, this chapter illustrated how city context is significantly related to the economic achievement of immigrants, from locational distribution, to the earnings of those participating in immigrant businesses, and to the racial and ethnic composition of neighborhoods.

Chapter 6 explored how immigrants influence cities, especially the city culture and the larger social structure, in the process of adapting to them. Specifically, it explored this two-way process of influence from the perspective of the foodscape, playscape, and landscape. With regard to the foodscape, traditional models of food being brought into enclaves and slowly becoming mainstream are still relevant, but suburbanization and socioeconomic diversity of immigrant groups have led to new forms of food and cuisine. Despite these changes, the process of introducing ethnic food into a host culture remains the same: it is one part of the more general process of adaptation and influence. Immigrants have been longstanding and successful entrepreneurs in the foodscape, as is clear from the long list of immigrant foods that are now mainstream.

With regard to the playscape, chapter 6 depicted the difficulty for immigrants to integrate with members of the host society in leisure activities. The extent of integration depends on a number of factors, including time in the country, social class, group size, discrimination, and especially mutual affinity for popular leisure pursuits, which can lead to connection or conflict depending on the context of the social contact. Leisure activities can represent important opportunities for forging social ties and mutual respect. However, they also sometimes maintain ethnic boundaries and solidarity, such as a subculture developing among co-ethnic immigrants based on a sport (e.g., cricket).

Chapter 6 concluded by showing how immigrants have influenced the development of current urban landscapes; their culture and identity transforms physical environments such as retail, commercial, suburban, and public spaces. Regardless of where immigrants settle, acts of place-making are visible everywhere. They can be seen in the built environment in distinctive forms of retail, signage, housing, monuments, festivals, and other activities. For example, suburban shopping centers built by Chinese-Canadian entrepreneurs have thrived in the "ethnoburbs," serving as essential centers of community life. Place-making is also seen in social rituals within public spaces, such as the collective performance of Italian immigrants' ritual evening walk through their neighborhood.

Chapter 7 explored how time-use data can help clarify the growing complexity of immigrant adaptation. These data can yield rich information about the lived experiences of immigrants in contemporary cities, as well as how daily life fosters and impedes acculturation and integration. It discussed three main aspects of time-use data and research as they relate to the immigrant experience. First, time-use data can be studied using both qualitative and quantitative approaches; together, these can yield rich information about what immigrants do with their time, with whom, and why. Second, time-use data can clarify how immigrant children adjust to a new society, often serving as bridges between their family's culture and the new culture. Third, these data can reveal how immigrant adults allocate their time to work, home, and community activities, and identify constraints such as commuting time that affect the time available for assimilating activities. Immigrant households often divide labor-market and household work in a way that is consistent with the "family investment" hypothesis: seeking to maximize future economic integration by investing in the human capital of household members with the most to gain. Immigrants are also less likely than native-born individuals to undertake multiple tasks at once (multi-tasking), potentially benefitting them through more concentrated effort, but also making it difficult for them to complete many tasks in a complex society.

Taken together, the analyses in this book have four major implications. First, it is clear that the adaptation processes and outcomes of immigrants in cities have become more complicated. No single perspective can explain immigrant residential patterns, and immigrant groups have a variety of trajectories in housing attainment. The functions of immigrant communities have also become more diverse: immigrant businesses now vary more than ever in terms of size, scale, and types of industry. This complexity is largely the result of the increasing racial and ethnic diversity of immigrants, their diverse socioeconomic backgrounds, and differences in cultural and economic development of their places of origin. As a result, existing models need to be re-evaluated and refined to ensure their applicability to specific immigrant groups.

The second implication is that the socioeconomic and demographic backgrounds of immigrants have strong influences on the processes of adaptation and acculturation, which in turn shape the urban form. This dynamic has been well documented since the early twentieth century, in research about residential patterns, housing attainment, and immigrant communities in general. However, classic and current models differ in two main ways. First, the processes and outcomes of adaptation and acculturation have become more complicated. Their effects on urban forms also vary greatly due to factors such as race, socioeconomic background, gender, and the internal cohesion and economic strategies of particular immigrant groups. Many immigrant groups experience starkly differing housing and settlement choices, reflecting their diverse origins. For example, ethnoburbs largely reflect the integration patterns of immigrants with more socioeconomic resources. The other difference between classic and current models is that more recent research has focused more on how the integration of immigrants influences a city's culture, foods, and leisure sports. For example, the presence of immigrants encourages ethnic and fusion cuisine, thereby enriching a city's cosmopolitan lifestyle.

The third implication is that urban forms shape the outcomes and processes of integration among immigrants. Housing availability affects housing attainment, and the analysis of ethnic enclaves and economies reveals how urban structures can significantly affect earnings for both entrepreneurs and employees. Additionally, the different socioeconomic and demographic characteristics of neighborhoods shape the locational distribution of immigrant businesses.

The fourth implication is that new measures and approaches are needed to better describe complex processes of adaptation and acculturation. Time-use data are one lens through which to observe the behavior and lived experience of contemporary immigrants, and how their lives vary from those of native-born residents. For example, immigrant children's dual role in a new society is illuminated by the time they spend as bridges between their family's culture and the new culture. Most immigrant children perform well in school, a finding underpinned by the time spent studying and engaging in organized educational activities.

In short, as immigrants settle in a city, their integration patterns and outcomes shape the city's development. At the same time, the forms of the host city shape their integration. This dual process creates a complex picture that is further obscured by increasing diversity and changes in urban structures. New forms of research, such as time-use data, can help clarify these fascinating developments.

Notes

Chapter 3: Housing Attainment, Ownership, and the Immigrant Experience in Global Cities

1 Chapter 7 examines how time-use data is useful for measuring the extent to which the actual behavior of immigrants is assimilated to that of natives. Much of the literature on immigrant time use deals with examining the differences between natives and immigrants – differences that often map out their contrasting sociocultural norms (Hossain and Shipman 2009; Ribar, 2012; van Klaveren et al., 2011; Zaiceva & Zimmermann, 2014).

Chapter 6: Immigrants and the Foodscapes, Playscapes, and Landscapes of Global Cities

1 Luis Wirth observed almost a century ago that one of the great values of urban life is its tendency to bring a diversity of ideas and influences together in ways that create better and more innovative life.

2 A current incarnation of creative urban elites is the notion of the "Creative Class" posited as a socioeconomic class by American economist and social scientist Richard Florida of the University of Toronto. The Creative Class includes people in science and engineering, architecture and design, education, arts, music, and entertainment whose economic function is to create new ideas, new technology, and new creative content.

3 The affinities of cultural omnivores are also significant as taste-makers driving aesthetic and cultural policy and development.

4 Transnational aspects of major employers in immigrant-intensive cities have an important influence on immigrants and their success (Morawska 2004). Multinational corporations are important to the economies of cities, but they are also powerful draws for talented immigrants (Li and Lo 2012). As evidence of their impact on these important employers in global cities, immigrants are more likely to sit in positions of influence within these organizations. At the

other end of the economic scale, immigrants also play an important role in the low-skill urban labor market (Liu 2013).

5 Ethnic cuisines have had a slow route to acceptance and status among other "national" cuisines. International migration has also had an important role in situating ethnic cuisine relative to national cuisine, such as in the case of the Chinese restaurant sector in Rome (Mudu 2007).

6 Other examples include Third and Fairfax Farmer's Market in Los Angeles, Twilight Hawkers Market in Perth, Australia, and Toronto's St. Lawrence Market.

7 The concept of symbolic power was first introduced by French sociologist Pierre Bourdieu to account for the tacit, almost unconscious modes of cultural/social domination occurring within the everyday social habits maintained over conscious subjects. Symbolic power accounts for discipline used against another to confirm that individual's placement in a social hierarchy.

8 Representing a flexible form of social space for immigrants, the emerging literature on "scenes" examines inventive forms of leisure created by ethnic minority immigrants in global cities. Kosnick (2012) focused on ethnic club "scenes" to explore how young post-migrants participate in forms of social engagement and cultural experimentation, within a context that is often at odds with their traditional identity and cultural views. "Scenes" are fluid social formations that are more permeable and temporary than traditional communities. Such spaces can be created and dissolved easily, lowering the costs and normative constraints on their existence. Disadvantaged migrant groups can create a kind of ownership over these social formations by producing culturally familiar experiences and different kinds of solidarity and encounters among disadvantaged groups.

References

Agrawal, Sandeep Kumar. 2006. "Housing Adaptations: A Study of Asian Indian Immigrant Homes in Toronto." *Canadian Ethnic Studies*, 38(1): 117–30.

Ahmed, Ali M., and Mats Hammarstedt. 2008. "Discrimination in the Rental Housing Market: A Field Experiment on the Internet." *Journal of Urban Economics*, 64(2): 362–72.

Alba, Richard D., and John R. Logan. 1991. "Variations on Two Themes: Racial and Ethnic Patterns in the Attainment of Suburban Residence." *Demography*, 28: 431–53.

Alba, Richard D., and John R. Logan. 1992. "Assimilation and Stratification in the Homeownership Patterns of Racial and Ethnic Groups." *International Migration Review*, 26(4): 1314–41.

Alba, Richard D., and Logan, John R. 1993. "Minority Proximity to Whites in Suburbs: An Individual-Level Analysis of Segregation." *American Journal of Sociology*, 98(6), 1388–427.

Alba, Richard, and Victor Nee. 2003. *Remaking the American Mainstream: Assimilation and Contemporary Immigration*. Cambridge, MA: Harvard University Press.

Aldrich, Howard E., and Albert J. Reiss. 1976. "Continuities in the Study of Ecological Succession: Changes in the Race Composition of Neighborhoods and Their Businesses." *American Journal of Sociology*, 81(4): 846–66.

Aldrich, Howard E., John Cater, and Trevor Jones. 1985. "Ethnic Residential Concentration and the Protected Market Hypothesis." *Social Forces*, 63: 996–1005.

Anastario, Michael, and Leah Schmalzbauer. 2008. "Piloting the Time Diary Method among Honduran Immigrants: Gendered Time Use." *Journal of Immigrant and Minority Health*, 10(5): 437–43.

Anderson, Kay. 1991. *Vancouver's Chinatown: Racial Discourse in Canada, 1875–1980*. Montreal: McGill-Queen's University Press.

References

Andersson, Roger. 2007. "Ethnic Residential Segregation and Integration Processes in Sweden." In Karen Schönwälder (ed.), *Residential Segregation and the Integration of Immigrants: Britain, the Netherlands and Sweden*. Berlin: WZB, pp. 61–90.

Arbel, Yuval, Danny Ben-Shahar, and Yossef Tobol. 2012. "The Correlation among Immigrant Homeownership, Objective and Subjective Characteristics, and Civic Participation: New Evidence from the Israeli Experience." *Urban Studies*, 49(11): 2479–99.

Bach, Jonathan. 2010. "'They Come in Peasants and Leave Citizens': Urban Villages and the Making of Shenzhen, China." *Cultural Anthropology*, 25(3): 421–58.

Bae, Chang-Hee Christine. 2004. "Immigration and Densities: A Contribution to the Compact Cities and Sprawl Debates." In Harry W. Richardson and Chang-Hee Christine Bae (eds.), *Urban Sprawl in Western Europe and the United States*. New York: Routledge, pp. 278–91.

Bailey, Trevor, and Tony Gatrell. 1995. *Interactive Spatial Data Analysis*. Harlow: Pearson.

Baker, Michael, and Dwayne Benjamin. 1997. "The Role of the Family in Immigrants' Labor-Market Activity: An Evaluation of Alternative Explanations." *American Economic Review*, 87(4): 705–27.

Basch, Linda, Nina, Glick Schiller and Cristina, Szanton Blanc. 1994. *Nations Unbound: Transnational Projects, Post-Colonial Predicaments and Deterritorialized Nation-States*. New York: Routledge.

Baxter, Jennifer. 2007. Children's Time Use in the Longitudinal Study of Australian Children: Data Quality and Analytical Issues in the 4-year Cohort. Technical Paper No. 4. Melbourne: Australian Institute of Family Studies.

Benford, Robert D., and David A. Snow. 2000. "Framing Processes and Social Movements: An Overview and Assessment." *Annual Review of Sociology*, 26(1): 611–39.

Berry, Brian J. L., and Philip H. Rees. 1969. "The Factorial Ecology of Calcutta." *American Journal of Sociology*, 74(5): 445–91.

Blalock, H. M. 1957. "Per Cent Non-White and Discrimination in the South." *American Sociological Review*, 22(6): 677–82.

Blazquez, Maite, Carlos Llano, and Julian Moral. 2010. "Commuting Times: Is There Any Penalty for Immigrants?" *Urban Studies*, 47(8): 1663–86.

Blomley, Nick K. 1997. "Property, Pluralism and the Gentrification Frontier." *Canadian Journal of Law and Society*, 12(2): 187–218.

Bobo, Lawrence, and Camille L. Zubrinsky. 1996. "Attitudes on Residential Integration: Perceived Status Differences, Mere In-Group Preference, or Racial Prejudice?" *Social Forces*, 74(3): 883–909.

Bonacich, Edna, and John Modell. 1980. *The Economic Basis of Ethnic Solidarity: Small Business in the Japanese American Community*. Berkeley, CA: University of California Press.

Borjas, George J. 2001. *Heaven's Door: Immigration Policy and the American Economy*. Princeton, NJ: Princeton University Press.

Borjas, George J. 2002. "Homeownership in the Immigrant Population." *Journal of Urban Economics*, 52(3): 448–76.

Bourassa, Steven C. 1994. "Immigration and Housing Tenure Choice in Australia." *Journal of Housing Research*, 5(1): 117–37.

Bourne, Larry S. 1997. "Social Polarization and Spatial Segregation: Changing Income Inequalities in Canadian Cities." In R. Davies (ed.) *Contemporary City Structuring*. Cape Town: University of Cape Town Press, pp. 134–47.

Breton, Raymond. 1964. "Institutional Completeness and the Personal Relations of Immigrants." *American Journal of Sociology*, 70(2): 193–205.

Breton, Raymond. 1991. *The Governance of Ethnic Communities: Political Structures and Processes in Canada*. New York: Greenwood Press.

Broda, Christian and David E. Weinstein. 2006. "Globalization and the Gains from Variety." *The Quarterly Journal of Economics*, 121(2): 541–85.

Bronfenbrenner, Urie. 1979. *The Ecology of Human Development*. Cambridge, MA: Harvard University Press.

Brosseau, Marc, Philippe Garvie, Liqiao Chen, and André Langlois. 1996. "Les méga-maisons de Kerrisdale, Vancouver: Chronique d'un quartier en transformation." *Le Géographe Canadien*, 40(2): 164–72.

Burgess, Ernest. 1925. "The Growth of the City: An Introduction to a Research Project." In Robert E. Park, Ernest W. Burgess, and Roderick D. McKenzie (eds.), *The City*. Chicago, IL: University of Chicago Press, pp. 47–62.

Buzzelli, Michael. 2001. "From Little Britain to Little Italy: An Urban Ethnic Landscape Study in Toronto." *Journal of Historical Geography*, 27(4): 573–87.

Carpusor, Adrian G., and William E. Loges. 2006. "Rental Discrimination and Ethnicity in Names." *Journal of Applied Social Psychology*, 36(4): 934–52.

Carter, Tom. 2005. "The Influence of Immigration on Global City Housing Markets: The Canadian Perspective." *Urban Policy and Research*, 23(3): 265–86.

Castles, Stephen, Hein de Haas, and Mark J. Miller. 2013. *The Age of Migration*, 5th edn. New York: Guilford Press.

Chao, Ruth K. 1994. "Beyond Parental Control and Authoritarian Parenting Style: Understanding Chinese Parenting through the Cultural Notion of Training." *Child Development*, 65(4): 1111–19.

Chao, Ruth K. 1996. "Chinese and European American Mothers' Beliefs about the Role of Parenting in Children's School Success." *Journal of Cross-Cultural Psychology*, 27(4): 403–23.

Charles, Camille Z. 2001. "Processes of Racial Residential Segregation." In Alice O'Connor, Chris Tilly, and Lawrence Bobo (eds.), *Urban Inequality: Evidence from Four Cities*. New York: Russell Sage Foundation.

Charles, Camille Z. 2006. *Won't You Be My Neighbor? Race, Class, and Residence in Los Angeles*. New York: Russell Sage Foundation.

Chen, Jen-Hao. 2014. "The Social Organization of Time-Use in Native and Immigrant Children." 2014 Annual Meeting, Population Association of America.

Chen, Wenhong, and Justin Tan. 2009. "Understanding Transnational Entrepreneurship through a Network Lens: Theoretical and Methodological Considerations." *Entrepreneurship Theory & Practice*, 33(5): 1079–91.

Chiang, Shiao-Yun, and Ho Hon Leung. 2011. "Making a Home in US Rural Towns: The Significations of Home for Chinese Immigrants' Work, Family and Settlement in Local Communities." *Community, Work & Family*, 14(4): 469–86.

Chiswick, Barry R. 1978. "The Effect of Americanization on the Earnings of Foreign-Born Men." *Journal of Political Economy*, 86(5): 897–921.

Clark, William A. V., and Valerie Ledwith. 2005. "How Much Does Income Matter in Neighborhood Choice?" 2004 Annual Meeting, Population Association of America.

Constant, Amelie F., Rowan Roberts, and Klaus F. Zimmermann. 2009. "Ethnic Identity and Immigrant Homeownership." *Urban Studies*, 46(9): 1879–98.

Coulson, N. Edward. 1999. "Why are Hispanic- and Asian-American Homeownership Rates So Low? Immigration and Other Factors." *Journal of Urban Economics*, 45(2): 209–27.

Cowen, Tyler. 2012. *An Economist Gets Lunch*. New York: E.P. Dutton & Co.

Crowder, Kyle, Matthew Hall, and Stewart E. Tolnay. 2011. "Neighborhood Immigration and Native Out-Migration." *American Sociological Review*, 76(1): 25–47.

Crowder, Kyle, Jeremy Pais, and Scott J. South. 2012. "Neighborhood Diversity, Metropolitan Constraints, and Household Migration." *American Sociological Review*, 77(3): 325–53.

Del Giudice, Luisa. 1993. "The "Archvilla": An Italian Canadian Architectural Archetype." In Luisa Del Giudice (ed.) *Studies in Italian American Folklore*. Logan, UT: Utah Press, pp. 53–105.

Delmelle, Elizabeth C. 2015. "Five Decades of Neighborhood Classifications and their Transitions: A Comparison of Four US Cities, 1970–2010." *Applied Geography*, 57: 1–11.

Denton, Nancy A., and Douglas S. Massey. 1991. "Patterns of Neighborhood Transition in a Multiethnic World: US Metropolitan Areas, 1970–1980." *Demography*, 28(1): 41–63.

Dietz, Robert D., and Donald R. Haurin. 2004. "The Social and Private Micro-Level Consequences of Homeownership." *Journal of Urban Economics*, 54(3): 401–50.

Dion, Kenneth 2001. "Immigrants' Perceptions of Housing Discrimination in Toronto: The Housing New Canadians Project." *Journal of Social Issues*, 57(3): 523–39.

Doherty, Alison. 2007. "Sport and Physical Recreation in the Settlement of Immigrant Youth." *Leisure/Loisir*, 31(1): 27–55.

Durington, Matthew. 2006. "Race, Space and Place in Suburban Durban: An Ethnographic Assessment of Gated Community Environments and Residents." *GeoJournal*, 66(1): 147–60.

Eger, Isaac. 2012. "'I Got Net': Exploring New York Through Pickup Basketball." *New York Times*, July 11.

Eggers, Mitchell L., and Douglas S. Massey. 1991. "The Structural Determinants of Urban Poverty: A Comparison of Whites, Blacks, and Hispanics." *Social Science Research*, 20: 217–55.

Elling, Agnes, and Inge Claringbould. 2005. "Mechanisms of Inclusion and Exclusion in the Dutch Sports Landscape: Who Can and Wants to Belong?" *Sociology of Sport Journal*, 22(4): 498–515.

Farley, Reynolds, and Walter Recharde Allen. 1990. "The Color Line and the Quality of Life in America (Book Review)." *Journal of the American Planning Association*, 56: 102–6.

Farley, Reynolds, Charlotte Steeh, and Maria Krysan. 1994. "Stereotypes and Segregation: Neighborhoods in the Detroit Area." *American Journal of Sociology*, 100(3): 750–80.

Farrer, James. 2010. "Eating the West and Beating the Rest: Culinary Occidentalism and Urban Soft Power in Asia's Global Food Cities." In James Farrer (ed.) *Globalization, Food and Social Identities in the Asia Pacific Region*. Tokyo: Sophia University Institute of Comparative Culture.

Firey, Walter. 1945. "Sentiment and Symbolism as Ecological Variables." *American Sociological Review*, 10(2): 140–8.

Fischer, Claude S. 1972. "Urbanism as a Way of Life." *Sociological Methods & Research*, 1(2): 187–242.

Fischer, Claude S. 1975. "Toward a Subcultural Theory of Urbanism." *American Journal of Sociology*, 80(6): 1319–41.

Fischer, Mary J., and Douglas S. Massey 2004. "The Ecology of Racial Discrimination." *City & Community*, 3(3): 221–41.

Florida, Richard. 2009. *Who's Your City: How the Creative Economy is Making Where to Live the Most Important Decision of Your Life*. Toronto: Random House of Canada.

Foner, Nancy. 1997. "The Immigrant Family: Cultural Legacies and Cultural Changes." *International Migration Review*, 31(4): 961–74.

Fong, Eric. 2013. "Partial Residential Integration: Suburban Residential Patterns of New Immigrant Groups in a Multiethnic Context." In Eric Fong, Nora Chiang, and Nancy Denton (eds.), *Immigrant Adaptation in Multi-Ethnic Societies: Canada, Taiwan, and the United States*. New York: Routledge, pp. 31–53.

Fong, Eric, and Elic Chan. 2010. "The Effect of Economic Standing, Individual Preferences, and Co-ethnic Resources on Immigrant Residential Clustering." *International Migration Review*, 44(1): 111–41.

Fong, Eric, and Elic Chan. 2011. "Residential Patterns among Religious Groups in Canadian Cities." *City & Community*, 10(4): 393–413.

Fong, Eric, and Feng Hou. 2009. "Residential Patterns across Generations of New Immigrant Groups." *Sociological Perspectives*, 52(3): 409–28.

Fong, Eric, and Linda Lee. 2007. "Chinese Ethnic Economies within the City Context." In Eric Fong and Chiu Luk (eds.), *Chinese Ethnic Business: Global and Local Perspectives*. London: Routledge, pp. 149–72.

Fong, Eric, and Emi Ooka. 2002. "The Social Consequences of Participating in Ethnic Economy." *International Migration Review*, 36(1): 125–46.

Fong, Eric, and Emi Ooka. 2006. "Patterns of Participation in Informal Social Activities among Chinese Immigrants in Toronto." *International Migration Review*, 40(2): 348–74.

Fong, Eric, and Jing Shen. 2011. "Explaining Ethnic Enclave, Ethnic Entrepreneurial and Employment Niches: A Case Study of Chinese in Canadian Immigrant Gateway Cities." *Urban Studies*, 48(8): 1605–34.

Fong, Eric, and Kumiko Shibuya. 2005. "Multiethnic Cities in North America." *Annual Review of Sociology*, 31: 285–84.

Fong, Eric, and Rima Wilkes. 1999. "An Examination of Spatial Assimilation Model." *International Migration Review*, 33(3): 594–620.

Fong, Eric, Emily E. Anderson, Wenhong Chen, and Chiu Luk. 2008. "The Logic of Ethnic Business Distribution in Multiethnic Cities." *Urban Affairs Review*, 43(4): 497–519.

Fong, Eric, Xingshan Cao, and Elic Chan. 2010. "Out of Sight, Out of Mind?: Patterns of Transnational Contact among Chinese and Indian Immigrants in Toronto." *Sociological Forum*, 25(3): 428–49.

Fong, Eric, Wenhong Chen, and Chiu Luk. 2012. "A Study of Locational Distribution of Small and Large Ethnic Businesses in a Multiethnic City: Chinese in Toronto, Canada." *Journal of Small Business Management*, 50(4): 678–98.

Fong, Eric, James Jeong, Alice Hoe, and Siyue Tian. 2015. "Earnings of Immigrant Entrepreneurs and Paid Workers in Canadian Gateway and Non-Gateway Metropolises." *Population Research and Policy Review*, 34(2): 279–305.

Fortin, Nicole M. 1995. "Allocation Inflexibilities, Female Labor Supply, and Housing Assets Accumulation: Are Women Working to Pay the Mortgage?" *Journal of Labor Economics*, 13(3): 524–57.

Fortin, Nicole M., David Green, Thomas Lemieux, and Craig Riddell. 2012. "Canadian Inequality: Recent Developments and Policy Options." *Canadian Public Policy*, 38(2): 121–45.

Frey, William H., and Reynolds Farley. 1996. "Latino, Asian, and Black Segregation in US Metropolitan Areas: Are Multiethnic Metros Different?" *Demography*, 33(1): 35–50.

Friesen, Joe, and Les Perreaux. 2013. "The Great Melting Rink." *The Globe and Mail*, May 21.

Frisby, Wendy. 2011. "Promising Physical Activity Inclusion Practices for Chinese Immigrant Women in Vancouver, Canada." *Quest*, 63(1): 135–47.

Gabaccia, Donna R. 2000. *We Are What We Eat: Ethnic Food and the Making of Americans*. Cambridge, MA: Harvard University Press.

Galster, George. 2001. "On the Nature of Neighbourhood." *Urban Studies*, 38(12): 2111–24.

Ghosh, Sutama. 2007. "Transnational Ties and Intra-Immigrant Group Settlement Experiences: A Case Study of Indian Bengalis and Bangladeshis in Toronto." *GeoJournal*, 68(2–3): 223–42.

Giuntella, Osea. 2012. "Do Immigrants Squeeze Natives Out of Bad Schedules? Evidence from Italy." *IZA Journal of Migration*, 1(1): 7.

Gobster, Paul H. 1998. "Explanations for Minority 'Underparticipation' in Outdoor Recreation: A Look at Golf." *Journal of Park and Recreation Administration*, 16(1): 46–64.

Gordon, Milton. 1964. *Assimilation in American Life: The Role of Race, Religion, and National Origins*. New York: Oxford University Press.

Gordon-Larsen, Penny, Kathleen Mullan Harris, Dianne S. Ward, and Barry M. Popkin. 2003. "Acculturation and Overweight-Related Behaviors among Hispanic Immigrants to the US: The National Longitudinal Study of Adolescent Health." *Social Science & Medicine*, 57(11): 2023–34.

Grey, Mark. 1992. "Sports and Immigrant, Minority and Anglo Relations in Garden City (Kansas) High School." *Sociology of Sport Journal*, 9(3): 255–70.

Haan, Michael. 2007. "The Homeownership Hierarchies of Canada and the United States: The Housing Patterns of White and Non-White Immigrants of the Past Thirty Years." *International Migration Review*, 41(2): 433–65.

Hall, Matthew. 2013. "Residential Integration on the New Frontier: Immigrant Segregation in Established and New Destinations." *Demography*, 50(5): 1873–96.

Hall, Suzanne M. 2011. "High Street Adaptations: Ethnicity, Independent Retail Practices and Localism in London's Urban Margins." *Environment and Planning A*, 34(11): 2571–88.

Hamermesh, Daniel S. and Stephen J. Trejo. 2010. "How Do Immigrants Spend Their Time? The Process of Assimilation." IZA Discussion Paper 5010, Institute for the Study of Labor, Bonn.

Hamermesh, Daniel S. and Stephen J. Trejo. 2013. "How Do Immigrants Spend Their Time? The Process of Assimilation." *Journal of Population Economics*, 26(2): 507–30.

Harney, Nicholas DeMaria. 2006. "The Politics of Urban Space: Modes of Place-Making by Italians in Toronto's Neighbourhoods." *Modern Italy*, 11(1): 25–42.

Hay, Roy. 1997. "Croatia: Community, Conflict and Culture: The Role of Soccer Clubs in Migrant Identity." In Mike Cronin and David Mayall (eds.), *Sporting*

Nationalisms: Identity, Ethnicity, Immigration and Assimilation. Portland, OR: Frank Cass.

He, Shenjing, Yuting Liu, Fulong Wu, and Chris Webster. 2010. "Social Groups and Housing Differentiation in China's Urban Villages: An Institutional Interpretation." *Housing Studies*, 25(5): 671–91.

Heimer, Carol A. 2007. "Old Inequalities, New Disease: HIV/AIDS in Sub-Saharan Africa." *Annual Review of Sociology*, 33(1): 551–77.

Hiebert, Daniel. 1999. "Immigration and the Changing Social Geography of Greater Vancouver." *BC Studies*, 121: 35–82.

Hin, Li Ling, and Li Xin. 2011. "Redevelopment of Urban Villages in Shenzhen, China – An Analysis of Power Relations and Urban Coalitions." *Habitat International*, 35(3): 426–34.

Hofferth, Sandra L., and Ui Jeong Moon. 2012. "Electronic Play, Study, Communication, and Adolescent Achievement, 2003 to 2008." *Journal of Research on Adolescence*, 22(2): 215–24.

Hofferth, Sandra L., and John F. Sandberg. 2001. "How American Children Spend Their Time." *Journal of Marriage and Family*, 63(2): 295–308.

Hogan, Bernie and Brent Berry. 2011. "Racial and Ethnic Biases in Rental Housing: An Audit Study of Online Apartment Listings." *City and Community*, 10(4): 351–71.

Horton, John. 1995. *The Politics of Diversity: Immigration, Resistance, and Change in Monterey Park, California*. Philadelphia, PA: Temple University Press.

Hossain, Ziarat, and Virginia Shipman. 2009. "Mexican Immigrant Fathers' and Mothers' Engagement with School-Age Children." *Hispanic Journal of Behavioral Sciences*, 31(4): 468–91.

Hou, Feng, and John Myles. 2005. "Neighbourhood Inequality, Neighbourhood Affluence and Population Health." *Social Science & Medicine*, 60(7): 1557–69.

Huang, Weishan. 2010. "Immigration and Gentrification – A Case Study of Cultural Restructuring in Flushing, Queens." *Diversities*, 12(1): 56–69.

Hulchanski, J. David. 2010. "The Three Cities within Toronto." Toronto, Canada: University of Toronto, Cities Centre. Available at: http://www.urbancentre.utoronto.ca/pdfs/curp/tnrn/Three-Cities-Within-Toronto-2010-Final.pdf

Hwang, Jackelyn. 2016. "Pioneers of Gentrification: Transformation in Global Neighborhoods in Urban America in the Late Twentieth Century." *Demography*, 53(1): 189–213.

Iceland, John, and Melissa Scopilliti. 2008. "Immigrant Residential Segregation in US Metropolitan Areas, 1990–2000." *Demography*, 45(1): 79–94.

Janson, Carl-Gunnar. 1980. "Factorial Social Ecology: An Attempt at Summary and Evaluation." *Annual Review of Sociology*, 6: 433–56.

Joesch, Jutta M. 1994. "Children and the Timing of Women's Paid Work after Childbirth: A Further Specification of the Relationship." *Journal of Marriage and the Family*, 56(2): 429–40.

Juster, F. Thomas, Hiromi Ono, and Frank P. Stafford. 2003. "An Assessment of Alternative Measures of Time Use." *Sociological Methodology*, 33(1): 19–54.

Kallick, David Dyssegaard. 2012. "Immigrant Small Business Owners." New York: US Fiscal Policy Institute's Immigration Research Initiative.

Kariv, Dafna, Teresa V. Menzies, and Gabrielle A. Brenner. 2010. "Business Success among Visible and Non-Visible Ethnic Entrepreneurs: A Look at the Effects of Unemployment, Co-Ethnic Involvement and Human Capital." *Global Business and Economics Review*, 12(1–2): 115–50.

Kasinitz, Philip, John H. Mollenkopf, Mary C. Waters, and Jennifer Holdaway. 2008. *Inheriting the City: The Children of Immigrants Come of Age*. Cambridge, MA: Harvard University Press.

Katz, I. and Gerry Redmond. 2010. "Review of the Circumstances among Children in Immigrant Families in Australia." *Child Indicators Research*, 3(4): 439–58.

Kennedy, Steven, James Ted McDonald, and Nicholas Biddle. 2006. "The Healthy Immigrant Effect and Immigrant Selection: Evidence from Four Countries." SEDAP Research Paper, 164, 2006–12.

Kim, Ann H., and Monica Boyd. 2009. "Housing Tenure and Condos: Ownership by Immigrant Generations and the Timing of Arrival." *Canadian Journal of Urban Research*, 18(1): 47–73.

Kitching, John, David Smallbone, and Rosemary Athayde. 2009. "Ethnic Diasporas and Business Competitiveness: Minority-Owned Enterprises in London." *Journal of Ethnic and Migration Studies*, 35(4): 689–705.

Kofman, Liz, and Suzanne Bianchi. 2012. "Time Use of US Immigrant and Native Born Youth." *Monthly Labor Review*, 135(6): 3–24.

Kosnick, Kira. 2012. "Ethnic Clubbing and Niche Entrepreneurialism in the European Metropolis." In Helmut K. Anheier and Yudhishthir Raj Isar (eds.), *Cultural Policy and Governance in a New Metropolitan Age*. London: Sage, pp. 56–8.

Krivo, Lauren J. 1995. "Immigrant Characteristics and Hispanic-Anglo Housing Inequality." *Demography*, 32(4): 599–615.

Krugman, Paul. 1979. "Increasing Returns, Monopolistic Competition, and International Trade." *Journal of International Economics*, 9: 469–79.

Krysan, Maria, Mick P. Couper, Reynolds Farley, and Tyrone Forman. 2009. "Does Race Matter in Neighborhood Preferences? Results from a Video Experiment." *American Journal of Sociology*, 115(2): 527–59.

Kwate, Naa Oyo A., Melody S. Goodman, Jerrold Jackson, and Julen Harris. 2013. "Spatial and Racial Patterning of Real Estate Broker Listings in New York City." *The Review of Black Political Economy*, 40(4): 401–24.

Kwong, Peter. 1996. *The New Chinatown*. New York: Hill and Wang.

Landale, Nancy S., and R. S. Oropesa. 2007. "Hispanic Families: Stability and Change." *Annual Review of Sociology*, 33: 381–405.

Landolt, Patricia. 2001. "Salvadoran Economic Transnationalism: Embedded Strategies for Household Maintenance, Immigrant Incorporation, and Entrepreneurial Expansion." *Global Networks*, 1(3): 217–42.

Lapointe Consulting, and Robert A. Murdie. 1996. *Immigrants and the Canadian Housing Market*. Ottawa: Canada Mortgage and Housing Corporation.

Lareau, Annette. 2011. *Unequal Childhoods: Class, Race, and Family Life*, 2nd edn. Berkeley, CA: University of California Press.

Larson, Reed W., and Suman Verma. 1999. "How Children and Adolescents Spend Time across the World: Work, Play, and Developmental Opportunities." *Psychological Bulletin*, 125(6): 701–36.

Laryea, Samuel A. 1999. "Housing Ownership Patterns of Immigrants in Canada." Working Paper No. 99-19. Vancouver: Research on Immigration and Integration in the Metropolis.

Lazear, Edward P. 2000. "Diversity and Immigration." In George J. Borjas (ed.), *Issues in the Economics of Immigration*. Chicago, IL: University of Chicago Press, pp. 117–42.

Lee, Barrett A., and Peter B. Wood. 1991. "Is Neighborhood Racial Succession Place-Specific?" *Demography*, 28(1): 21–40.

Lee, Jennifer, and Min Zhou. 2014. "The Success Frame and Achievement Paradox: The Costs and Consequences for Asian Americans." *Race and Social Problems*, 6(1): 38–55.

Lee, Jo-Anne and Veronica Pacini-Ketchabaw. 2011. "Immigrant Girls as Caregivers to Younger Siblings: A Transnational Feminist Analysis." *Gender and Education*, 23(2): 105–19.

Ley, David. 2005. "The Social Geography of the Service Economy in Gateway Cities." In Peter W. Daniels, Kong Chong Ho and Tom Hutton (eds.) *Service Industries and Asia-Pacific Cities*. London: Routledge, pp. 77–92.

Ley, David. 2010. *Millionaire Migrants: Trans-Pacific Life Lines*. Oxford: Wiley-Blackwell.

Ley, David, and Heather Smith. 2000. "Relations between Deprivation and Immigrant Groups in Large Canadian Cities." *Urban Studies*, 37(1): 37–62.

Li, Peter S. 2001. "Immigrants' Propensity to Self-Employment: Evidence from Canada." *International Migration Review*, 35(4): 1106–28.

Li, Peter S., and Yahong Li. 1999. "The Consumer Market of the Enclave Economy: A Study of Advertisements in a Chinese Daily Newspaper in Toronto." *Canadian Ethnic Studies*, 31(2): 43–60.

Li, Wei. 1998a. "Anatomy of a New Ethnic Settlement: the Chinese Ethnoburb in Los Angeles." *Urban Studies*, 35(3): 479–501.

Li, Wei. 1998b. "Los Angeles' Chinese Ethnoburb: From Ethnic Service Center to Global Economy Outpost." *Urban Geography*, 19(6): 502–17.

Li, Wei, and Lucia Lo. 2012. "New Geographies of Migration?: A Canada-US Comparison of Highly Skilled Chinese and Indian Migration." *Journal of Asian American Studies*, 15(1): 1–34.

Lieberson, Stanley. 1963. *Ethnic Patterns in American Cities*. Glencoe, IL: The Free Press.

Light, Ivan. 2006. *Deflecting Immigration: Networks, Markets and Regulation in Los Angeles*. New York: Russell Sage Foundation.

Light, Ivan Hubert, and Steven J. Gold. 2000. *Ethnic Economies*. San Diego, CA: Academic Press.

Liu, Cathy Yang. 2013. "Latino Immigration and the Low-Skill Urban Labor Market: The Case of Atlanta." *Social Science Quarterly*, 94(1): 131–57.

Liu, Yansui, Yu Liu, Yangfen Chen, and Hualou Long. 2010a. "The Process and Driving Forces of Rural Hollowing in China under Rapid Urbanization." *Journal of Geographical Sciences*, 20(6): 876–88.

Lo, Lucia and Shuguang Wang 1997. "Settlement Patterns of Toronto's Chinese Immigrants: Convergence or Divergence?" *Canadian Journal of Regional Science/Revue canadienne des sciences régionales*, 20(1–2): 49–72.

Logan, John R., and Richard D. Alba. 1999. "Minority Niches and Immigrant Enclaves in New York and Los Angeles: Trends and Impacts." In Frank D. Bean and Stephanie Bell-Rose (eds.), *Immigration and Opportunity: Race, Ethnicity, and Employment in the United States*. New York: Russell Sage Foundation, pp. 173–293.

Logan, John R., and Harvey Molotch. 2007. *Urban Fortunes: The Political Economy of Place*. Berkeley, CA: University of California Press.

Logan, John R., and Charles Zhang. 2010. "Global Neighborhoods: New Pathways to Diversity and Separation." *American Journal of Sociology*, 115(4): 1069–109.

Logan, John R., Richard D. Alba, and Thomas L. McNulty. 1994. "Ethnic Economies in Metropolitan Regions: Miami and Beyond." *Social Forces*, 72(3): 691–798.

Logan, John R., Wenquan Zhang, and Richard D. Alba. 2002. "Immigrant Enclaves and Ethnic Communities in New York and Los Angeles." *American Sociological Review*, 67(2): 299–322.

Long, James E. 1980. "The Effect of Americanization on Earnings: Some Evidence for Women." *Journal of Political Economy*, 88(3): 620–9.

MacLachlan, Ian and Ryo Sawada. 1997. "Measures of Income Inequality and Social Polarization in Canadian Metropolitan Areas." *The Canadian Geographer/Le Géographe canadien*, 41(4), 377–97.

Magnusson Turner, L., and Lina Hedman. 2014. "Linking Integration and Housing Career: A Longitudinal Analysis of Immigrant Groups in Sweden." *Housing Studies*, 29(2): 270–90.

Marshall, Nancy L., Cynthia Garcia Coll, Fern Marx, Kathleen McCartney, Nancy Keefe, and Jennifer Ruh. 1997. "After-School Time and Children's Behavioral Adjustment." *Merrill Palmer Quarterly*, 43(3): 497–514.

Marshall, Simon J., Deborah A. Jones, Barbara E. Ainsworth, Jared P. Reis, Susan S. Levy, and Caroline A. Macera. 2007. "Race/Ethnicity, Social Class, and Leisure-Time Physical Inactivity." *Medicine and Science in Sports Exercise*, 39: 44–51.

Martinovic, Borja. 2009. "Dynamics of Interethnic Contact: A Panel Study of Immigrants in the Netherlands." *European Sociological Review*, 25(3): 303–18.

Massey, Douglas S., and Nancy A. Denton. 1988a. "Suburbanization and Segregation in US Metropolitan Areas." *American Journal of Sociology*, 94(3): 592–626.

Massey, Douglas S., and Nancy A. Denton. 1988b. "The Dimensions of Residential Segregation." *Social Forces*, 67(2): 281–315.

Massey, Douglas S., and Nancy A. Denton. 1990. "American Apartheid: Segregation and the Making of the Underclass." *American Journal of Sociology*, 96(2): 329–57.

Massey, Douglas S., and Eric Fong. 1990. "Segregation and Neighborhood Quality: Blacks, Hispanics, and Asians in the San Francisco Metropolitan Area." *Social Forces*, 69(1): 15–32.

Massey, Douglas S., and Brendon P. Mullan. 1984. "Process of Hispanic and Black Spatial Assimilation." *American Journal of Sociology*, 39(4): 836–73.

Massey, Douglas S., Gretchen A. Condran, and Nancy A. Denton. 1987. "The Effect of Residential Segregation on Black Social and Economic Well-Being." *Social Forces*, 66(1): 29–56.

Massey, Douglas, Rafael Alarcón, Jorge Durand, and Humberto González. 1990. *Return to Aztlan: The Social Process of International Migration from Western Mexico*. Berkeley, CA: University of California Press.

Massey, Douglas S., Andrew B. Gross, and Kumiko Shibuya. 1994. "Migration, Segregation, and the Geographic Concentration of Poverty." *American Sociological Review*, 59(3): 425–45.

Massey, Douglas S., Camille Z. Charles, Garvey F. Lundy, and Mary J. Fischer. 2006. *The Source of the River: The Social Origins of Freshmen at America's Selective Colleges and Universities*. Princeton, NJ: Princeton University Press.

Maxim, Paul S. 1992. "Immigrants, Visible Minorities, and Self-Employment." *Demography*, 29(2): 181–98.

Mazzolari, Francesca. 2012. "Immigration and Product Diversity." *Journal of Population Economics*, 25(3): 1107–37.

Mazzolari, Francesca and David Neumark. 2012. "Immigration and Product Diversity." *Journal of Population Economics*, 25(3): 1107–37.

Mendez, P., Hiebert, D., and Wyly, E. 2006. "Landing at Home: Insights on Immigration and Metropolitan Housing Markets from the Longitudinal Survey of Immigrants to Canada." *Canadian Journal of Urban Research*, 15: 82–104.

Mensah, Joseph, and Christopher J. Williams. 2014. "Cultural Dimensions of African Immigrant Housing in Toronto: A Qualitative Insight." *Housing Studies*, 29(3): 438–55.

Messner, Steven F., and Luc Anselin. 2004. "Spatial Analyses of Homicide with Areal Data." In Michael F. Goodchild and Donald G. Janelle (eds.), *Best Practices in Spatially Integrated Social Science*. New York: Oxford University Press, pp. 127–44.

Min, Pyong Gap. 1996. *Caught in the Middle: Korean Merchants in America's Multiethnic Cities*. Berkeley, CA: University of California Press.

Min, Pyong Gap. 2008. *Ethnic Solidarity for Economic Survival: Korean Greengrocers in New York*. New York: Russell Sage Foundation.

Morawska, Ewa. 2004. "Immigrant Transnational Entrepreneurs in New York." *International Journal of Entrepreneurial Behaviour & Research*, 10(5): 325–48.

Mudu, Pierpaolo. 2007. "The People's Food: The Ingredients of 'Ethnic' Hierarchies and the Development of Chinese Restaurants in Rome." *GeoJournal*, 68(2–3): 195–210.

Müller, Floris, Liesbet van Zoonen, and Laurens de Roode. 2008. "The Integrative Power of Sport: Imagined and Real Effects of Sport Events on Multicultural Integration." *Sociology of Sport Journal*, 25(3): 387–401.

Murdie, Robert A. 2008. "Diversity and Concentration in Canadian Immigration: Trends in Toronto, Montréal and Vancouver, 1971–2006." Toronto: Centre for Urban and Community Studies (Cities Centre), Research Bulletin 42.

Murdie, Robert A., Adrienne Chambron, J. David Hulchanski, and Carlos Teixeira. 1996. "Housing Issues Facing Immigrants and Refugees in Greater Toronto: Initial Findings from the Jamaican, Polish and Somali Communities." In E.M. Komut (ed.) *The Housing Question of the "Others"*. Ankara: Chamber of Architects of Turkey, pp. 179–90.

Musterd, Sako, and Wim Ostendorf. 2007. "Spatial Segregation and Integration in the Netherlands." In Karen Schönwälder (ed.), *Residential Segregation and the Integration of Immigrants: Britain, the Netherlands and Sweden*. Berlin: WZB.

Myers, Dowell. 2001. "Demographic Futures as a Guide to Planning: California's Latinos and the Compact City." *Journal of the American Planning Association*, 67(4): 383–97.

Myers, Dowell, and Seong Woo Lee. 1998. "Immigrant Trajectories into Homeownership: A Temporal Analysis of Residential Assimilation." *International Migration Review*, 32(3): 593–625.

Myles, John, and Feng Hou. 2003. "Neighbourhood Attainment and Residential Segregation among Toronto's Visible Minorities." Statistics Canada – Analytical Studies Branch Research Paper. Catalogue # 11F0019MIE – No. 206.

Myles, John, and Feng Hou. 2004. "Changing Colours: Spatial Assimilation and New Racial Minority Immigrants." *Canadian Journal of Sociology*, 29(1): 29–58.

Nee, Victor, Jimy M. Sanders, and Scott Sernau. 1994. "Job Transitions in an Immigrant Metropolis: Ethnic Boundaries and the Mixed Economy." *American Sociological Review*, 59(6): 849–72.

Novac, Sylvia, Joe Darden, David Hulchanski, and Anne-Marie Séguin. 2002. "Housing Discrimination in Canada: What Do We Know about It?" CUCS Research Bulletin no. 11 (summary of CMHC report). Toronto: Centre for Urban and Community Studies, University of Toronto.

Ogbu, John U. 1995. "Cultural Problems in Minority Education: Their Interpretations and Consequences." *Urban Review*, 27(3): 271–97.

Ogbu, John U. 2008. *Minority Status, Oppositional Culture and Schooling*. New York: Routledge.

Okamoto, Dina. 2003. "Toward a Theory of Panethnicity: Explaining Asian American Collective Action." *American Sociological Review*, 68(6): 811–42.

Oliver, J. Eric. 2010. *The Paradoxes of Integration: Race, Neighborhood, and Civic Life in Multiethnic America*. Chicago, IL: University of Chicago Press.

Olzak, Susan. 1992. *The Dynamics of Ethnic Competition and Conflict*. Stanford, CA: Stanford University Press.

Ooka, Emi, and Barry Wellman. 2006. "Does Social Capital Pay Off More Within or Between Ethnic Groups? Analyzing Job Searchers in Five Toronto Ethnic Groups." In Eric Fong (ed.), *Inside the Mosaic*. Toronto: University of Toronto Press, pp. 199–226.

Orellana, Marjorie F. 2001. "The Work Kids Do: Mexican and Central American Immigrant Children's Contributions to Households and Schools in California." *Harvard Educational Review*, 71(3): 366–89.

Orrenius, Pia M. and Madeline Zavodny. 2009. "The Effects of Tougher Enforcement on the Job Prospects of Recent Latin American Immigrants." *Journal of Policy Analysis and Management*, 28(2): 239–57.

Osili, Una Okonkwo, and Jia Xie. 2009. "Do Immigrants and Their Children Free Ride More Than Natives?" *American Economic Review*, 99(2): 28–34.

Owusu, Thomas Y. 1998. "To Buy Or Not To Buy: Determinants of Home Ownership among Ghanaian Immigrants in Toronto." *The Canadian Geographer/Le Géographe Canadien*, 42(1): 40–52.

Pacione, Michael. 2009. *Urban Geography: A Global Perspective*, 3rd rev. edn. New York: Routledge.

Painter, Gary, Lihong Yang, and Zhou Yu. 2004. "Homeownership Determinants for Chinese Americans: Assimilation, Ethnic Concentration and Nativity." *Real Estate Economics*, 32(3): 509–39.

Pais, Jeremy F., and James R. Elliott. 2008. "Places as Recovery Machines: Vulnerability and Neighborhood Change After Major Hurricanes." *Social Forces*, 86(4): 1415–54.

Park, Kyeyoung. 1997. *The Korean American Dream: Immigrants and Small Business in New York City*. Ithaca, NY: Cornell University Press.

Park, Robert E. 1936a. "Succession, An Ecological Concept." *American Sociological Review*, 1(2): 171–9.
Park, Robert E. 1936b. "Human Ecology." *American Journal of Sociology*, 42(1): 1–15.
Pascali, Lara. 2006. "Two Stoves, Two Refrigerators, Due Cucine: The Italian Immigrant Home with Two Kitchens." *Gender, Place & Culture*, 13(6): 685–95.
Passel, Jeffrey S. 2011. "Demography of Immigrant Youth: Past, Present, and Future." *The Future of Children*, 21(1): 19–42.
Persons, Stow. 1987. *Ethnic Studies at Chicago, 1905–45*. Urbana, IL: University of Illinois Press.
Pescador, Juan Javier. 2004. "¡Vamos Taximaroa! Mexican/Chicano Soccer Associations and Transnational/Translocal Communities, 1967–2002." *Latino Studies*, 2(3): 352–76.
Po, Lanchih. 2011. "Property Rights Reforms and Changing Grassroots Governance in China's Urban-Rural Peripheries: The Case of Changping District in Beijing." *Urban Studies*, 48(3): 509–28.
Portes, Alejandro. 1981. "Modes of Structural Incorporation and Present Theories of Labor Immigrations." In Mary M. Kritz, Charles B. Keely, and Silvano M. Tomasi (eds.), *Global Trends in Migration*. Staten Island, NY: CMS Press, pp. 279–97.
Portes, Alejandro. 2014. "Downsides of Social Capital." *Proceedings of the National Academy of Sciences of the United States of America*, 111(52): 18407–8.
Portes, Alejandro, and Robert Bach. 1985. *Latin Journey: Cuban and Mexican Immigrants in the United States*. Berkeley, CA: University of California Press.
Portes, Alejandro, and Ruben G. Rumbaut. 2006. *Immigrant America: A Portrait*. Los Angeles, CA: University of California Press.
Portes, Alejandro, and Julia Sensenbrenner. 1993. "Embeddedness and Immigration: Notes on the Social Determinants of Economic Action." *American Journal of Sociology*, 98(6): 1320–50.
Portes, Alejandro, and Min Zhou. 1993. "The New Second Generation: Segmented Assimilation and Its Variants." *Annals of the American Academy of Political and Social Sciences*, 530: 74–96.
Portes, Alejandro, Luis Eduardo Guarnizo, and William J. Haller. 2002. "Transnational Entrepreneurs: An Alternative Form of Immigrant Economic Adaptation." *American Sociological Review*, 67(2): 278–98.
Portes, Alejandro, Cristina Escobar, and Alexandria Walton Radford. 2007. "Immigrant Transnational Organizations and Development: A Comparative Study." *International Migration Review*, 41(1): 248–81.
Preston, Valerie, and Lucia Lo. 2000. "'Asian theme' Malls in Suburban Toronto: Land Use Conflict in Richmond Hill. *The Canadian Geographer*, 44(2): 182–90.

Preston, Valerie, Sara McLafferty, and Xiao Feng Liu. 1998. "Geographical Barriers to Employment for American-Born and Immigrant Workers." *Urban Studies*, 35(3): 529–45.

Preston, Valerie, Robert Murdie, and Ann Marie Murnaghan. 2007. "The Housing Situation and Needs of Recent Immigrants in the Toronto CMA." CERIS Working Paper No. 56.

Putnam, Robert D. 2000. *Bowling Alone: The Collapse and Revival of American Community*. New York: Simon & Schuster.

Ramey, David M. 2013. "Immigrant Revitalization and Neighborhood Violent Crime in Established and New Destination Cities." *Social Forces*, 92(2): 597–629.

Ray, Brian K. 1998. *A Comparative Study of Immigrant Housing, Neighbourhoods and Social Networks in Toronto and Montréal*. Ottawa: Canada Mortgage and Housing Corporation.

Ribar, David C. 2012. "Immigrants' Time Use: A Survey of Methods and Evidence." IZA Discussion Papers 6931, Institute for the Study of Labor (IZA), Bonn.

Rogoff, Barbara. 2003. *The Cultural Nature of Human Development*. New York: Oxford University Press.

Rose, John. 1999. "Immigration, Neighbourhood Change, and Racism: Immigrant Reception in Richmond, B.C." Vancouver: RIIM Working Paper #99-15.

Rumbaut, Rubén G. 2008. "Reaping What You Sew: Immigration, Youth, and Reactive Ethnicity." *Applied Developmental Science*, 22(2): 1–4.

Ryan, Camille L., and Kurt Bauman. 2016. "Educational Attainment in the United States: 2015." Current Population Reports. Washington, DC: US Department of Commerce, US Census Bureau. Available at: www.census.gov/content/dam/Census/library/publications/2016/demo/p20-578.pdf

Saiz, A. 2007. "Immigration and Housing Rents in American Cities." *Journal of Urban Economics*, 61(2): 345–71.

Sampson, Robert J. 2012. *Great American City: Chicago and the Enduring Neighborhood Effect*. Chicago, IL: University of Chicago Press.

Sampson, Robert J., Stephen W. Raudenbush, and Felton Earls. 1997. "Neighborhoods and Violent Crime: A Multilevel Study of Collective Efficacy." *Science*, 277(5328): 918–24.

Sanders, Jimy, and Victor Nee. 1987. "Limits of Ethnic Solidarity in the Enclave Economy." *American Sociological Review*, 52(6): 745–67.

Sarroub, Loukia K. 2001. "The Sojourner Experience of Yemeni American High School Students: An Ethnographic Portrait." *Harvard Education Review*, 71(3): 390–415.

Saxenian, AnnaLee, and Jumbi Edulbehram. 1997. "Immigrant Entrepreneurs in Silicon Valley." *Berkeley Planning Journal*, 12(1): 32–49.

Schieman, Scott. 2005. "Residential Stability and the Social Impact of

Neighborhood Disadvantage: A Study of Gender- and Race-Contingent Effects." *Social Forces*, 83(3): 1031–64.

Schoeni, Robert F. 1998. "Labor Market Outcomes of Immigrant Women in the United States: 1970 to 1990." *International Migration Review*, 32(1): 57–77.

Scott, Allen J. 2000. *The Cultural Economy of Cities: Essays on the Geography of Image-Producing Industries*. New York: Sage.

Simone, Dylan, and K. Bruce Newbold. 2014. "Housing Trajectories Across the Urban Hierarchy: Analysis of the Longitudinal Survey of Immigrants to Canada, 2001–2005." *Housing Studies*, 29(8): 1096–116.

Singer, Audrey. 2008. "Twenty-First Century Gateways: An Introduction." In Audrey Singer, Susan W. Hardwick, and Caroline B. Brettell (eds.), *Twenty-First Century Gateways: Immigrant Incorporation in Suburban America*. Washington, DC: Brookings Institution Press, pp. 3–30.

Singer, Audrey. 2013. "Contemporary Immigrant Gateways in Historical Perspective." *Daedalus*, 142(3): 76–91.

Sinning, M. 2010. "Homeownership and Economic Performance of Immigrants in Germany." *Urban Studies*, 47(2): 387–409.

Small, Mario Luis. 2002. "Culture, Cohorts, and Social Organization Theory: Understanding Local Participation in a Latino Housing Project." *American Journal of Sociology*, 108(1): 1–54.

Small, Mario Luis. 2009. *Unanticipated Gains: Origins of Network Inequality in Everyday Life*. New York: Oxford University Press.

Smith, Judith R., Jeanne Brooks-Gunn, and Pamela K. Klebanov. 1997. "Consequences of Living in Poverty for Young Children's Cognitive and Verbal Ability and Early School Achievement." In Greg J. Duncan, and Jeanne Brooks-Gunn (eds.), *Consequences of Growing Up Poor*. New York: Russell Sage Foundation, pp. 132–89.

Smith, Sandra Susan. 2005. "'Don't Put My Name On It': Social Capital Activation and Job-Finding Assistance among the Black Urban Poor." *American Journal of Sociology*, 111(1): 1–57.

Søholt, S. 2014. "Pathways to Integration: Cross-Cultural Adaptations to the Housing Market in Oslo." *Journal of Ethnic and Migration Studies*, 40(10): 1637–56.

South, Scott J., and Kyle D. Crowder. 1997. "Escaping Distressed Neighborhoods: Individual, Community, and Metropolitan Influences." *American Journal of Sociology*, 102(4): 1040–84.

South, Scott J., and Kyle D. Crowder. 1998. "Leaving the 'Hood: Residential Mobility between Black, White, and Integrated Neighborhoods." *American Sociological Review*, 63(1): 17–26.

Statistics Canada. 1996. "1996 Census Table: Selected demographic, cultural, educational, labour force and income characteristics (207) of the total population by age groups (6) and sex (3), showing visible minority population (14) (20% sample) (94F0009XDB96003)."

Statistics Canada. 2008. "2006 Census Table: Visible Minority Groups (15) X Age Groups (10) and Sex (3) (97-562-xcb2006009)."

Statistics Canada. 2013. "Immigration and Ethnocultural Diversity in Canada." Analytical Document: National Household Survey, 2011.

Stodolska, Monika. 1998. "Assimilation and Leisure Constraints: Dynamics of Constraints on Leisure in Immigrant Populations." *Journal of Leisure Research*, 30(4): 521–51.

Stodolska, Monika, and Konstantinos Alexandris. 2004. "The Role of Recreational Sport in the Adaptation of First Generation Immigrants in the United States." *Journal of Leisure Research*, 36(3): 379–413.

Stoll, Michael A., and Janelle S. Wong. 2007. "Immigration and Civic Participation in a Multiracial and Multiethnic Context." *International Migration Review*, 41(4): 880–908.

Suttles, Gerald D. 1968. *The Social Order of the Slum: Ethnicity and Territory in the Inner City*. Chicago, IL: University of Chicago Press.

Taverno, Sharon E., Brandi Y. Rollins, and Lori A. Francis. 2010. "Generation, Language, Body Mass Index, and Activity Patterns in Hispanic Children." *American Journal of Preventive Medicine*, 38(2): 145–53.

Taylor, Denise S., Valerie K. Fishell, Jessica L. Derstine, Rebecca L. Hargrove, Natalie R. Patterson, Kristin W. Moriarty, Beverly A. Battista, Hope E. Ratcliffe, Amy E. Binkoski, and Penny M. Kris-Etherton. 2000. "Street Foods in America – A True Melting Pot". In Artemis P. Simopoulos and Ramesh Venkataramana Bhat (eds.) *Street Foods*. Basel: Karger, pp. 25–44.

Teixeira, Carlos. 2007. "Residential Experiences and the Culture of Suburbanization – A Case Study of Portuguese Homebuyers in Mississauga." *Housing Studies*, 22(4): 495–521.

Teixeira, Carlos. 2008. "Barriers and Outcomes in the Housing Searches of New Immigrants and Refugees: A Case Study of 'Black' Africans in Toronto's Rental Market." *Journal of Housing and the Built Environment*, 23: 253–76.

Terriquez, Veronica. 2011. "Schools for Democracy: Labor Union Participation and Latino Immigrant Parents' School-Based Civic Engagement." *American Sociological Review*, 76(4): 581–601.

Thomas, William T., and Florian Znaniecki. 1995. *The Polish Peasant in Europe and America*. Champaign, IL: University of Illinois Press.

Tirone, Susan. 1999. "Racism, Indifference, and the Leisure Experiences of South Asian Canadian Teens." *Leisure/Loisir*, 24(1–2): 89–114.

Toussaint-Comeau, Maude, and Sherrie L. W. Rhine. 2000. *Ethnic Immigrant Enclaves and Homeownership: A Case Study of an Urban Hispanic Community*. Chicago, IL: Federal Reserve Bank of Chicago.

Trouille, David. 2013. "Neighborhood Outsiders, Field Insiders: Latino Immigrant Men and the Control of Public Space." *Qualitative Sociology*, 36(1): 1–22.

Turcotte, Martin. 2008. "The Difference between City and Suburb: How Can We Measure It?" *Canadian Social Trends*, 85. Catalogue no. 11-008-XIE, Ottawa: Minister of Industry.

Vallejo, Jody Agius. 2009. "Latina Spaces: Middle-Class Ethnic Capital and Professional Associations in the Latino Community." *City & Community*, 8(2): 129–54.

Van Hook, Jennifer, Susan L. Brown, and Maxwell Ndigume Kwenda. 2004. "A Decomposition of Trends in Poverty among Children of Immigrants." *Demography*, 41(4): 649–70.

van Klaveren, Chris, Bernard M. S. van Praag, and Henriette Maassen van den Brink. 2011. "Collective Labor Supply of Native Dutch and Immigrant Households in the Netherlands." In José Alberto Molina (ed.), *Household Economic Behaviors*. New York: Springer, pp. 99–119.

Vargas, Andreas. 2016. "Assimilation Effects beyond the Labor Market: Time Allocations of Mexican Immigrants to the US." *Review of Economics of the Household*, 14(3): 625–68.

Villarreal, Andrés, and Bráulio F.A. Silva. 2006. "Social Cohesion, Criminal Victimization and Perceived Risk of Crime in Brazilian Neighborhoods." *Social Forces*, 84(3): 1725–53.

Waldinger, Roger. 1986. *Through the Eye of the Needle: Immigrants and Enterprise in New York's Garment Trades*. New York: New York University Press.

Waldinger, Roger David, and Michael Ira Lichter. 2003. *How the Other Half Works: Immigration and the Social Organization of Labor*. Berkeley, CA: University of California Press.

Walks, R. Alan, and Larry S. Bourne. 2006. "Ghettos in Canadian Cities? Racial Segregation, Ethnic Enclaves and Poverty Concentration in Canadian Urban Areas." The Canadian Geographer, 50(3): 273–97.

Wang, Shuguang. 1996. "New Development Patterns of Chinese Commercial Activity in the Toronto CMA." Research Report 3. Toronto: Centre for the Study of Commercial Activity, Ryerson Polytechnic University.

Wang, Shuguang. 1999. "Chinese Commercial Activity in the Toronto CMA: New Development Patterns and Impacts." *The Canadian Geographer*, 43(1): 19–35.

Wang, Ya Ping, Yanglin Wang, and Jiansheng Wu. 2009. "Urbanization and Informal Development in China: Urban Villages in Shenzhen." *International Journal of Urban and Regional Research*, 33(4): 957–73.

Watson, James (ed.) 2006. *Golden Arches East: McDonald's in East Asia*, 2nd edn. Stanford: Stanford University Press.

Werbner, Pnina. 2001. "Metaphors of Spatiality and Networks in the Plural City: A Critique of the Ethnic Enclave Economy Debate." *Sociology*, 35(3): 671–93.

White, Michael J. 1988. *American Neighborhoods and Residential Differentiation*. New York: Russell Sage Foundation.

Wilson, Franklin D. 1999. "Ethnic Concentrations and Labor-Market Opportunities." In Frank D. Bean and Stephanie Bell-Rose (eds.), *Immigration and Opportunity: Race, Ethnicity, and Employment in the United States*. New York: Russell Sage Foundation, pp. 106–40.

Wilson, Franklin D. 2003. "Ethnic Niching and Metropolitan Markets." *Social Science Research*, 32: 429–66.

Wilson, Kenneth, and Alejandro Portes. 1980. "Immigrant Enclaves: An Analysis of the Labor Market Experiences of Cubans in Miami." *American Journal of Sociology*, 86(2): 295–319.

Wilson, William J. 1987. *The Truly Disadvantaged: The Inner City, the Underclass, and Public Policy*. Chicago, IL: University of Chicago Press.

Wilson, William J. 1996. *When Work Disappears: The World of the New Urban Poor*. New York: Knopf.

Wimmer, Andreas. 2008. "Elementary Strategies of Ethnic Boundary Making." *Ethnic and Racial Studies*, 31(6): 1025–55.

Wirth, Louis. 1962. *The Ghetto*. Chicago, IL: University of Chicago Press.

World Bank. 2015. Urban Population: Overview per Country. Available at: http://data.worldbank.org/indicator/SP.URB.TOTL.IN.ZS

Wu, Yuanlai, and Xianhui Hu. 2011. "Analysis on the Reform and Problems of Property Right System of Rural Residential Land by Local Government in the Process of Urbanization." Proceedings of the 2nd International Conference on Engineering and Business Management, March 22–24, pp. 2832–8.

Wu, Zheng, Feng Hou, and Christoph M. Schimmele. 2011. "Racial Diversity and Sense of Belonging in Urban Neighborhoods." *City & Community*, 10(4): 373–92.

Xie, Yu, and Margaret Gough. 2011. "Ethnic Enclaves and the Earnings of Immigrants." *Demography*, 48(4): 1293–315.

Yan, Jin H., and Penny McCullagh. 2004. "Cultural Influence on Youth's Motivation of Participation in Physical Activity." *Journal of Sport Behavior*, 27(4): 378–90.

Yang, You-Ren, and Hung-Kai Wang. 2007. "Land Property Rights Regimes in China: A Comparative Study of Suzhou and Dongguan." In Fulong Wu (ed.), *China's Emerging Cities*. London: Routledge, pp. 26–44.

Yoon, In-Jin. 1997. *On My Own: Korean Businesses and Race Relations in America*. Chicago, IL: University of Chicago Press.

Zacharias, John P. 1997. "The Redevelopment of Fairview Slopes in Vancouver, 1975–95." *Urban History Review*, 26(1): 32–42.

Zaiceva, Anzelika, and Klaus F. Zimmermann. 2011. "Do Ethnic Minorities 'Stretch' their Time? UK Household Evidence on Multitasking." *Review of Economics of the Household*, 9(2): 181–206.

Zaiceva, Anzelika, and Klaus F. Zimmermann. 2014. "Children, Kitchen, Church: Does Ethnicity Matter?" *Review of Economics of the Household*, 12(1): 83–103.

Zhao, Yanjing, and Chris Webster. 2011. "Land Dispossession and Enrichment in China's Suburban Villages." *Urban Studies*, 48(3): 529–51.

Zhou, Min. 1992. *Chinatown: The Socioeconomic Potential of an Urban Enclave*. Philadelphia, PA: Temple University Press.

Zhou, Min. 1997. "Segmented Assimilation: Issues, Controversies, and Recent Research on the New Second Generation." *International Migration Review*, 31(4): 825–58.

Zhou, Min, and Carl L. Bankston. 1994. "Social Capital and the Adaptation of the Second Generation: The Case of Vietnamese Youth in New Orleans." *International Migration Review*, 28(4): 821–45.

Zhou, Min, and Carl L. Bankston. 1998. *Growing Up American: How Vietnamese Children Adapt to Life in the United States*. New York: Russell Sage Foundation.

Zhou, Min, and John R. Logan. 1989. "Returns on Human Capital in Ethnic Enclaves: New York City's Chinatown." *American Sociological Review*, 54(5): 809–20.

Zong, Jie, and Jeanne Batalova. 2015. "Frequently Requested Statistics on Immigrants and Immigration in the United States." Washington, DC: Migration Policy Institute. Available at: http://www.migrationpolicy.org/article/frequently-requested-statistics-immigrants-and-immigration-united-states-4

Index

Index